W9-BYC-332

Best-loved Bible Stories

Best-loved Bible Stories from the New Testament

World Book–Childcraft International, Inc.
A subsidiary of The Scott & Fetzer Company
Chicago London Paris Sydney Tokyo Toronto

Merchandise Mart Plaza, Chicago, Illinois 60654

Printed in the United States of America
ISBN 0–7166–2059–6
Library of Congress Catalog Card No. 79–55309

Consultants

Michael Brooks
Program of Studies in Religion
University of Michigan
Ann Arbor, Michigan

Rev. Dr. Jack B. Van Hooser
Professor of Old Testament Literature and Languages
Seabury Western Theological Seminary
Evanston, Illinois

Rev. Donald Senior, C.P.
Associate Professor of New Testament Studies
Catholic Theological Union at Chicago
Chicago, Illinois

Staff

Editorial director
William H. Nault

Editorial

Executive editor
Robert O. Zeleny

Managing editor
Dominic J. Miccolis

Senior editor
Seva Johnson

Editors
Patricia R. Dragisic
Ellen Thanas

Editorial assistant
Janet T. Peterson

Writers
Lewis Donelson
Ruth Hallman
Ruth Hooker
Stella Pevsner
Berniece Rabe
DeVere M. Ramsay
Foster Stockwell

Index editor
Mary Kay Ellis

Art

Executive art director
William Dobias

Art director
William Hammond

Design director
Ronald A. Stachowiak

Senior designer
Free Chin

Production artists
Hans Bobzien
Susan T. Wilson

Contributing artist
George Suyeoka

Pre-press services

Director
J. J. Stack

Composition
John Babrick

Film separations
Alfred J. Mozdzen
Barbara J. McDonald

Production control
Janice Rossing
Barbara Podczerwinski

Editorial research

Jo Ann McDonald, *Head*
Yogamani Leo Hamm
Max R. Kinsey

Manufacturing

Philip B. Hall, *Director*
Joseph C. LaCount
Henry Koval

Contents

Events from New Testament times

These New Testament events are ranked in the order traditionally assigned to them. Dates for many of the historically verifiable events from the Bible are disputed among Biblical scholars. For our events from the New Testament, most dates are from *The World Book Encyclopedia.* The abbreviation *c.* stands for *circa,* or "about." The dates with *c.* in front of them are approximate.

Birth of John the Baptist (c. 7 BC)

Birth of Jesus (before 4 BC)

Jesus speaks with rabbis in Jerusalem (c. AD 6*)

Baptism of Jesus by John in Jordan River (27**)

Jesus is tempted in wilderness

Jesus' ministry begins in Galilee

Calling of apostles

Sermon on the Mount

Healings and feedings

Death of John

Jesus attends Passover in Jerusalem

Last Supper

Betrayal by Judas

Arrest and conviction by Pilate

Crucifixion (30**)

Pentecost (30)

Birth of the Christian Church

Christian missions begin

Death of Stephen

Paul converts (30s)

Paul visits Jerusalem leaders

Paul begins missionary journeys

Apostolic Council with Paul, Peter, James, John and others (c. 49)

*All dates to follow are AD.

**This date is disputed.

Paul in Corinth (c. 51)

Paul arrested
in Jerusalem (c. 58)

Paul tried before Festus (c. 60)

Paul's possible death
in Rome under Nero (late 60s)

War between Jews and Romans (66–70)

Christians in Jerusalem flee to Pella

Galilee captured by Vespasian (67)

Jerusalem captured by Titus
and destroyed (70)

Political rulers

	Rome	**Palestine**
37 BC		Herod the Great
27	Augustus	
4		Archelaus* Herod Antipas**
AD 6		Roman procurators* (Pontius Pilate 26–36)
14	Tiberius	
37	Caligula	
41	Claudius	Herod Agrippa I*
44		Roman procurators* (Felix 52–c. 59, Festus c. 59–62)
54	Nero	
68–69	Vespasian	

*Only of Judea.
**Only of Galilee (4 BC–AD 39).

Memorable figures from the New Testament

Abraham, called the "father of nations," is the ancestor of the people of Israel. His story appears in the Old Testament, but he is so important in the history of the Jews, his name also often appears in the New Testament. For more details about this great leader, see the entry **Abraham** in the Old Testament volume. In the New Testament volume, he is mentioned on pages 20–26, 49–56, 191–99.

Andrew, a fisherman from Bethsaida, was one of the original twelve apostles of Jesus. He was also the brother of another apostle, Simon Peter. Pp. 76–85, 110–18, 143–52, 181–90.

Barabbas was a rebel condemned to die on the cross. Pontius Pilate released him from jail and crucified Jesus in Barabbas' place upon the request of the crowd gathered at Jesus' trial. Pp. 161–80, 191–99.

Bartholomew was one of the original twelve apostles of Jesus. He came from the city of Cana in Galilee. Tradition says he carried the gospel to India and died a martyr there. Pp. 110–18, 143–52.

Caiaphas, a Pharisee, was the high priest of the Jews. He presided at the council that sent Jesus to Pontius Pilate, the Roman governor, for trial. Pp. 124–33, 153–70, 181–90.

King David was a shepherd boy from Bethlehem who became king of Israel. His name is often mentioned in connection with the Messiah. David was one of Israel's greatest kings, a great warrior. Many of the Jews hoped that the Messiah would be like King David and run the Romans, their rulers, out of Palestine.

Jesus' earthly father, Joseph, was one of David's descendants. When

Jesus' followers hailed him as the Son of David, they were referring to King David, Jesus' ancestor. See the entry **King David** in the Old Testament volume for details about this great king. In the New Testament volume, he is mentioned on pages 20–38, 49–56, 64–70, 134–42, 191–99.

Elijah was a prophet of Israel during the ninth century BC. Although his story takes place during Old Testament times, his name often appears in the New Testament, where he is noted as one of the great prophets. Both Elijah and Moses come back from death to appear to Jesus, Peter, James, and John. See the entry **Elijah** in the Old Testament volume for details about this prophet. In the New Testament volume, he is mentioned on pages 49–56 and 110–18.

Elizabeth was Zachariah's wife and the mother of John the Baptist. She was also a relative of Mary of Nazareth, Jesus' mother. Pp. 20–38.

Gabriel was the angel of God who appeared to Mary of Nazareth to tell her she would give birth to Jesus. Gabriel also was the angel who came to Zachariah to announce the coming birth of John the Baptist. Pp. 20–38.

The Good Samaritan was a man Jesus described as being a good neighbor. Samaritans were generally disliked by the Hebrews, who considered the Samaritans' religion inferior and refused to associate with them. Yet, the Good Samaritan stopped to help a wounded Jew who had been robbed and beaten. Pp. 95–99.

Herod Antipas, son of King Herod the Great, ruled in Palestine from AD 4–39. His wife Herodias hated John the Baptist and saw to it that Herod threw John into prison. Later, Herodias' daughter also forced Herod to have John beheaded. Pp. 57–63, 161–70.

King Herod the Great ruled in Palestine from about 37–4 BC. He had ten wives and many children, one of whom was Herod Antipas. Herod the Great was terribly cruel. He killed some of his own sons for rebelling against him. Herod also ordered the massacre of all the male children of Bethlehem after the birth of Jesus. To protect Jesus, Mary and Joseph fled to Egypt. They did not return until King Herod had died. Pp. 27–48, 57–63.

Herodias was the wife of Herod Antipas' brother. Herod fell in love with her, divorced his own wife, and married Herodias. John the Baptist publicly criticized Herodias and Herod for their marriage, and Herodias hated John. Finally, she arranged to have John beheaded. Pp. 57–63.

Isaiah was a great prophet of Judah. His story takes place in the Old Testament times, but his name also often appears in the New Testament. For more details about this great prophet, see the entry **Isaiah** in the Old Testament volume. In the New Testament volume, he is mentioned on pages 49–63, 153–60.

James is the name of two, and possibly three, persons in the New Testament. Saint James the Greater was the older brother of another apostle, John, and the first apostle to be martyred. Saint James the Less is listed as one of the original apostles in Matthew 10:3. In other parts of the Bible, he is identified with James, "the brother of the Lord," and James, the son of Mary, wife of Cleophas. Bible authorities interpret these passages differently. Pp. 76–85, 110–18, 153–60, 181–90.

Jesus was the founder of the Christian religion. Christians believe he is the Son of God, sent to earth to save humankind. There are many arguments over the exact date of his birth, but many scholars agree that he was born in Bethlehem sometime before 4 BC. He was crucified when he was in his thirties.

During his lifetime, Jesus was known as a preacher and a worker of miracles, a gentle master who cured the sick, raised the dead, and taught about a new way to God. His work took him to Jerusalem and to many parts of Galilee.

The New Testament calls Jesus by many names: the Christ, the Messiah, the Lamb of God, the Savior, the Son of David, and the King of the Jews, among others. Since our New Testament stories are devoted to the life of Jesus, you will find him throughout the pages of this volume.

John was one of the most loyal of the twelve original apostles of Jesus. A fisherman, he became a close companion of Jesus from the beginning of his ministry. John, known as the Apostle of Love, attended the trial of Jesus, was present when Jesus was crucified, and accepted the responsibility of caring for Jesus' mother Mary after Jesus' death. James, another apostle, was John's brother. Pp. 110–18, 134–60, 171–90.

John the Baptist was a great prophet who came before Jesus and announced the coming of the Messiah. He was the son of Zachariah and Elizabeth, one of Mary of Nazareth's relatives. John is also known as the Prophet of the Highest and the Forerunner, or the one who came before the Messiah. Herod Antipas, at the request of his wife Herodias' daughter, beheaded John after imprisoning him. Pp. 20–26, 49–70.

Joseph of Arimathea was a wealthy Pharisee who, with Nicodemus, spoke up for Jesus at his hearing before the Jewish council. After Jesus had died on the cross, Joseph asked Pontius Pilate for the body. With Nicodemus and some of Jesus' followers, Joseph buried the body in a newly built tomb that Joseph had bought for his own burial. Pp. 161–70, 181–90.

Joseph of Nazareth was the husband of Mary, the mother of Jesus. Joseph was a carpenter by trade. Pp. 27–48, 143–52.

Judas Iscariot, the treasurer of the apostles, betrayed Jesus to his enemies for thirty pieces of silver. With a kiss, Judas identified Jesus in the Garden of Gethsemane. Later, Judas hanged himself. Pp. 110–18, 124–33, 143–70.

Jude was one of the original twelve apostles of Jesus. He was also known as Lebbaeus or Thaddeus. He was not the Judas who betrayed Jesus. Pp. 110–18.

Lazarus was the brother of Mary and Martha of Bethany and a close friend of Jesus. When Lazarus became ill and died, Jesus came to his tomb and ordered him to rise, alive, from death. Pp. 119–42.

Malchus was the servant of Caiaphas, the high priest of Jerusalem. In a brief struggle during Jesus' arrest in the Garden of Gethsemane, Simon Peter cut off Malchus' ear. Jesus then healed Malchus. Pp. 153–60.

Martha of Bethany, a splendid housekeeper, was the sister of Mary and Lazarus, the man Jesus ordered to rise from the dead. Jesus often visited their home, and Martha did many things to provide comfort for him. Pp. 119–42.

Mary of Bethany, a devoted believer in Jesus, was the sister of Martha and Lazarus, the man Jesus ordered to rise from the dead. Jesus stayed in their home many times, and Mary sat listening to his teachings while her sister provided for his comfort. Before Jesus' death, Mary anointed Jesus' feet with precious oil. This act was one incident that caused Judas to betray Jesus to his enemies. Pp. 119–42.

Mary of Nazareth was Jesus' mother and the wife of Joseph of Nazareth. She gave birth to Jesus in a stable in Bethlehem. Mary is also known as the Virgin Mary, the Blessed Virgin Mary, and the Blessed Virgin. Pp. 20–48, 64–75, 171–90.

Mary Magdalene was a devoted follower of Jesus. She was named for the village of Magdala, where she was born. She stood at the cross when Jesus was crucified and was the first person to see him after he rose from death. Pp. 181–90.

Matthew, a publican, or professional tax collector, was one of the original twelve apostles of Jesus. Pp. 110–18, 143–52.

Micah was a prophet who lived during the time of King Hezekiah and the prophet Isaiah. He foretold of the coming of the Messiah, saying that the Son of God would someday be born in Bethlehem. Pp. 27–38.

Moses was a great leader chosen by God to take the Israelites out of Egypt and away from slavery. His story takes place during Old Testament times, but his name also often appears in the New Testament. Both Moses and Elijah came back from death to appear to Jesus, Peter, James, and John. See the entry **Moses** in the Old Testament volume for details about this great Israelite leader. In the New Testament volume, he is mentioned on pages 110–18, 143–52, 191–99.

Nicodemus was a Pharisee who, with Joseph of Arimathea, spoke up for Jesus at his hearing before the Jewish council. Later, Nicodemus helped Joseph and some of Jesus' followers bury Jesus' body in Joseph's tomb. Pp. 86–94, 161–70, 181–90.

Paul is known as the Apostle of the Gentiles, though he was not one of the original twelve apostles. He was one of the greatest preachers and organizers of the early Christian church, and he had much to do with spreading the new religion. Before Paul became a Christian, he was a Pharisee known as Saul. Born in Tarsus, he was the son of wealthy Jewish parents. Pp. 191–99.

Peter, or Simon Peter, was the leading member of the original twelve apostles of Jesus. Before he joined Jesus, he was a fisherman who lived in Bethsaida. His brother, Andrew, was also an apostle. Simon Peter was known as Peter the Rock. Pp. 76–94, 105–18, 143–70, 181–90.

Philip of Bethsaida was one of the original twelve apostles of Jesus. After Jesus' death, Philip went to Phrygia as a missionary and died there a martyr. Pp. 110–18.

Pontius Pilate was the Roman governor in Jerusalem who sentenced Jesus when he came to Roman trial. Pilate believed that Jesus was innocent, but the governor condemned him to the cross when Jesus' enemies demanded his death. Pp. 143–52, 161–90.

Salome was the daughter of Herodias and the stepdaughter of Herod Antipas, governor of Galilee. She is the young woman who is said to have caused the beheading of John the Baptist. The story of John's death appears on pages 57–63. **Salome** is also the name of one of the women present at the crucifixion and the resurrection of Jesus. This Salome was the mother of the apostles John and James the Greater. Pp. 181–90.

Satan was the evil spirit who tempted Jesus to turn away from God. This figure appears throughout the Bible. In the New Testament, Satan is also called by the names *devil, enemy,* and *Beelzebub.* See the entry **Satan** in the Old Testament volume for details about the nature of this character in earlier Bible stories. In the New Testament volume, Satan appears in the story on pages 64–70.

Saul is the Jewish name for Paul, called the Apostle of the Gentiles. For details about this apostle, see the entry **Paul.**

Simeon was a devout Jew who worshipped at the temple in Jerusalem. God had promised him that he would see the Messiah before he died. When Simeon was very old, Mary and Joseph of Nazareth brought Baby Jesus to the temple in Jerusalem for a religious ceremony. Simeon, seeing the child, hailed him as the Messiah. Pp. 39–48.

Simon was one of the twelve original apostles of Jesus. He is sometimes known as Simon the Zealot. This name sets him apart from another apostle, Simon Peter. Pp. 110–18, 134–52. **Simon** is also the name of a man who lived in Bethany. At his own house, Simon of Bethany held the final dinner that Jesus and his apostles shared with his friends Mary, Martha, and Lazarus. During this meal, Judas, voicing the viewpoint of other apostles, objected when Mary anointed Jesus' feet with precious oil. Pp. 124–33.

Simon of Cyrene made the long journey from his home in Africa to Jerusalem to celebrate the Passover the same year that Jesus died on the cross. The African was a bystander when, on the way to Calvary, Jesus fell a third time under the weight of his heavy crossbar. Roman soldiers forced Simon to carry the crossbar part of the way to Calvary, where Jesus died. Pp. 171–80.

Solomon was king of Israel when it reached its greatest wealth and glory. King Solomon is not an actual character in any of the New Testament stories. He is, however, referred to from time to time because of his famed riches and extravagant way of living, which Jesus taught against. For more details about this great king, see the entry **Solomon** in the Old Testament volume. In the New Testament volume, he is mentioned on pages 64–70, 110–18.

Thomas, also known as Doubting Thomas, was, despite that name, one of the most loyal of the twelve original apostles of Jesus. He is called "Doubting Thomas" because he said he would believe Jesus had risen from the dead only when he could touch the wounds Jesus had received on the cross. Pp. 110–18, 143–52, 181–90.

The Three Wise Men are said to have followed the course of a spectacular star to bring gifts to Baby Jesus. According to tradition, their names were Melchior, Balthasar, and Gaspar. There is, however, no certainty that these were their real names, nor that it was three wise men who visited Jesus. Pp. 27–48.

Zachariah, a devout Jew, and his wife Elizabeth became John the Baptist's parents when they were very old. The angel Gabriel visited Zachariah in a temple to tell him of the coming birth. Pp. 20–26.

John, Prophet of the Messiah

A little boy, with chubby brown legs churning, scooted down the hill. He came to a stop at the garden's edge, in back of Zachariah and Elizabeth's house. Elizabeth dusted his seat with a swat, gave him a sweet cake, and sent him scurrying to his own house.

Zachariah turned away from the longing he saw in his wife's face. They had been together for many years. Earlier in their marriage, there had still been hope for a child of their own. He had often prayed for a chance to serve as priest inside the Holy Place in the temple. Maybe there God would send a messenger to hear Zachariah's desperate prayer for a child.

People had always said that angels sometimes came to the temple. They also spoke of the coming of the Messiah and of his forerunner, the one who would announce that the Messiah would soon be among them. But these predictions were over four hundred years old. Still, the faithful believed the predictions would come true.

Zachariah himself was one of the faithful. He humbly served as a priest in what was called the course of Abijah. King David had established twenty-four courses, or kinds, of priest. Each course served, in turn, one week at the temple. This coming week was the turn for the course of Abijah to serve. Zachariah had noticed Elizabeth holding herself proudly as she helped him to prepare.

News moved fast in this little hill town in Judea. Everyone knew which men would be serving this week in the temple. Elizabeth happily smiled at her neighbors as she busied herself, pouring the water for Zachariah's bath. Wives of other priests did as Elizabeth, and there were thousands of other priests.

According to tradition, Zachariah had to prepare carefully for his week of service. He would stay absolutely clean, bathing frequently, and he would eat only the foods that were allowed according to custom. He would also stay away from wine. It was all part of the ceremony.

Elizabeth belonged to the family of Aaron, a priestly family. She knew the ceremonies well. During these times of service, she felt a fine sense of belonging. "The Lord blessed me when He gave you to me as my wife," said Zachariah.

The smile on Elizabeth's face broadened but then quickly left. It was as if the shadows that moved over the hills so quickly at twilight had come over her now at midday. How often she had felt the sting of her neighbors' words when they whispered that she was barren, that she had no children. How often she had felt that she was no blessing to Zachariah at all because she had never brought a child into their home. Her hands touched the wrinkles on her face as she said, "My dream of giving you a child has gone away. My life will end without ever being complete."

"Elizabeth, my dear wife, do not speak of that now," said Zachariah. "Please don't dwell on it. My heart aches as does yours, but let us find pleasure in the things that fill our lives. The will of God, we must accept. The fact that we are old—that, too, we must accept."

With one finger, Elizabeth traced the pattern on the water jug. "You have your calling. And—I do rejoice with you. But I cannot help but mourn my own lack. I accept the will of God, but to do so is sometimes hard."

"Hush," Zachariah told her. "You are a good wife. I know I can go to live within the temple for a whole week, leaving you by yourself to watch over our home. It comforts me that I can trust all in your care." Zachariah held her heavily veined hand a moment longer and then left to begin his duties.

The selection was soon to be made of the priests who would go into the temple to perform the day's holy services. Zachariah hurried, not wanting to be late. As he had done many times before, he watched the selection process. Lots were cast. And, on this day, the lot to light the incense fell to Zachariah. To perform his duty, he would have to enter the Holy Place, where the incense was always burned. "The Holy Place," Zachariah thought. "What a shame. If only this had happened in my youth. Then I could have stood before the golden altar and cried out to the Lord for a child. Now I am an old man with a wife past the age when she can have children."

Zachariah knew he should not go on thinking this way. He had to attend to the ceremony and forget his lost dreams. Humbly, he entered the Holy Place of the temple.

A great veil, over thirty feet high and made of the finest cloth, faced him. With the tiniest stitches, loving hands had sewn patterns on the veil. Beyond it was the Holy of Holies, a place where God Himself was always present. There, all the priests were forbidden to go.

Zachariah became more and more excited. Supposing an angel came? How would Zachariah act? He was fidgety, wishing that an angel would come and, at the same time, afraid of not knowing what to do if one did appear.

In his mind, Zachariah repeated the holy words as he carefully began to light the seven branches of the candlestick. On the table, he placed twelve loaves of shewbread. This was the bread that the priests would eat at the end of the week's service. Zachariah wanted to do his job well. Live coals had to glow upon the altar, and small, rocklike pieces of sweet-smelling incense were to be placed upon the coals to melt.

From behind the divider that separated the Holy Place from the temple courtyard, he could hear the people. They stood with their heads bowed in prayer. They were waiting for the clouds of smoke from the burning incense to appear above the altar, over the place where Zachariah worked.

Finally, Zachariah's work was complete. But he waited another moment for the smoke to rise into the view of those who prayed outside. Then he would walk out, bless them, and help deliver the closing prayer. The great honor of serving in the Holy Place was almost over.

But what was that? Something was moving to the right of the golden altar. Was it drifting smoke? No! It was a figure, a heavenly being, an angel. A great fear fell upon Zachariah. Breathing became difficult, and the smell of the incense was suddenly sharp and biting. A soft, mellow voice comforted him. "Fear not, Zachariah. I am bringing you a message from God. Your wife Elizabeth will bear you a son. You are to name him John. And not only will you and your wife be happy at his birth, but many people will rejoice with you.

"John will be one of the Lord's great ones, a man unlike others. He will be filled with the Holy Spirit from the moment of birth, and he will touch the hearts of many. John will turn the people toward their God. He will be called John the Forerunner and John the Baptist, and he will prepare the people for the Messiah's coming."

Zachariah did not know how to answer. The Messiah's forerunner was to be his and Elizabeth's son? "But how can this be?" Zachariah's words came in a great rush. "Can't you see? I am an old man, and my wife is old, too."

The angel's voice lost some of its gentleness. "I am Gabriel. I stood in the presence of God to hear this good news that I now bring to you. Because you will not believe it, you will be stricken, you will be left unable to speak until what I have told you does, indeed, happen."

God had made His will known. Zachariah stood bowed and silenced with awe. Everything was possible for God. Had He not blessed Sarah, Abraham's wife, so that in spite of her barrenness and old age, she had given birth to Isaac? Oh, how could Zachariah, who said he was a believer, have doubted a messenger from God? He looked up to beg forgiveness, but the angel was gone.

Outside in the temple courtyard, the people were growing restless. Zachariah had to go out to help deliver the closing prayer. He did so, but when it was his time to speak, no words came. He was mute. The Lord had silenced his tongue. Zachariah raised his hand towards the heavens. Heads began to nod. The people understood. They knew that on this day, in the Holy Place in the temple, a messenger from God had come. Filled with happiness, Zachariah watched the people scatter toward the village to spread the news.

Poor Zachariah! Mute, he still had to serve out the rest of his week's duty as a priest in the temple. When the week finally ended, Zachariah went to Elizabeth. He wrote the words of the angel Gabriel for her to behold.

Faithful Elizabeth did not doubt the angel's message. "How kind is the Lord," she said. "Now I, like other women, will have a child!"

When the day of birth at last arrived, Elizabeth and Zachariah became the parents of a healthy boy. Eight days later, they prepared for a celebration. On this day, the baby would be circumcised, a ritual that would rid him of uncleanliness and prepare him to become a true member of Israel. Also, the baby, on this day, would receive his name.

Neighbors fluttered about, helping the mother. "We must have the cloth clean and white for your little Zachariah," said one.

"I've brought nuts for the feast. Only the best for your little Zachariah," said another.

Elizabeth smiled and let them chatter. But when yet another said, "Zachariah, what a special baby you are to bless this home and carry on the name of your father after his death," Elizabeth felt she must speak out.

"No, he will be called John."

"What?" the neighbors exclaimed, as if with one voice. "Custom says that the son of Zachariah, his first son and no doubt his only son, must be named after his own father. We'd better ask Zachariah about this."

A great commotion followed. Men and women alike clustered around Zachariah, explaining the problem that Elizabeth was causing. Zachariah motioned for a writing tablet. On it, he wrote, "His name is John."

As he lay aside the tablet, the people cried out, "What is this? John? Zachariah agrees with Elizabeth? What manner of child is this?"

Zachariah felt the gift of speech return, and the words he had held within now could be shouted out in answer to the questions. He looked towards the heavens and declared, "Blessed be the Lord God of Israel, Who through His prophets made known the coming of a forerunner to the Messiah, who will save our people from our enemies.

"So be it. This child will be called the Prophet of the Highest. He will teach the mercy of the Lord. He will walk before the Son of God, the light that is soon to come to us who sit in the darkness, the light that will guide us towards peace."

Zachariah felt that the prayer he could not give that day at the temple had at last been given: a great closing prayer for what had started on that day. It was a prayer given by Zachariah the Believer, the blessed father of John.

So it was that many people rejoiced with him. And, even as they rejoiced, Mary of Nazareth, who was Elizabeth's cousin, was waiting to bring the light from heaven into the world.

Baby Jesus lights up the world

In Nazareth, Mary's family was still excited over the news. Her cousin Elizabeth, whom everyone thought was too old to have children, was pregnant. It seemed to be a miracle. Many people were wondering aloud if this special child might be the long-awaited Messiah.

Mary had heard many times in her short life about the Messiah, the one God was going to send to save Israel. The country buzzed with excitement every time any strange event occurred. Someone was always sure to say it was a sign from God, a sign that He was sending the Messiah.

But the Messiah had not come, not yet. In fact, no one even knew what kind of person he would be. A warrior—like Joshua? A king—like David? No one knew.

In the street in front of Mary's house, two Roman soldiers walked by. They were tall and strong. Their swords hung at their sides. They looked around without fear, for they knew they were the law in Israel. No Jew would dare harm them. But Mary was afraid as she looked at them. She thought, "Maybe the Messiah will be a warrior and will drive these foreign soldiers out of my country."

Then Mary turned away from the street and shook her head. She thought, "I am just a young girl. It is not right for me to wonder about the Messiah. Perhaps a learned person will find the truth, but not me. Anyway, I am a lucky young girl. I am engaged to Joseph, a fine man. We will be married soon. God has already given me enough."

Mary was alone in the house, busy with her work. Then, suddenly, she felt someone was in the room with her.

In front of Mary stood an angel. He was shining with heavenly light. He looked at her and called out, "I am Gabriel. I am here to tell you, 'Greetings, favored one. God is with you.' "

Mary was completely silent. She did not know what to think or what to say. She wondered, "Why is this angel, this messenger from God, here? And what does he mean by calling me 'favored one'?" But she said nothing aloud.

Then Gabriel spoke to her again, "Mary, do not be afraid. I am bringing you wonderful news. You have been chosen by God for a special task. You will now become pregnant, pregnant with a son. And, when he is born, you will call him Jesus."

The angel's voice was soothing, and somehow Mary was not afraid. She listened carefully to the angel.

"Your son will be great. He will be called the Son of God. And God will give to him the throne of David the King. And yet, your son will be greater than David, for his rule will never end. His kingdom will last forever."

"Forever?" thought Mary. "Is the angel talking about the Messiah?" But she did not speak these thoughts to the angel, for she was confused about something else.

Mary asked, "But how can I give birth to a son? I am not married. I am only engaged."

The angel's voice was kind as he answered Mary's question. "God will send His own spirit to you, and that spirit will make you pregnant. You do not need a husband, for God will be Jesus' father. Do not think that God cannot do this. Remember your cousin Elizabeth who, though old, is now pregnant. With God, nothing is impossible."

With these words the angel disappeared. Mary was alone again. But now everything had changed. She sat quietly, wondering, "Am I to be the mother of the Messiah?" Mary did not know what to think. But she remembered the angel's words: "With God, nothing is impossible."

Mary tried to continue her work, but her mind kept wandering to the angel's words. She walked slowly across the dirt floor to the other corner of the house, where the oven was warm from baking bread. As she pulled the bread from the oven, she smiled with satisfaction at its brown glow. She thought, "Joseph will like my cooking."

But then she stopped. She had forgotten about Joseph. What would she tell him? Would he believe such a story?

When Joseph found out that Mary was pregnant, he decided he would break their engagement quietly. He still loved Mary and he did not want to hurt her, but he decided he could not marry her if she was pregnant.

But one night when Joseph was sleeping, an angel appeared to him in a dream and said, "Joseph, do not be afraid to wed Mary. For the child within her has come from the Holy Spirit. She will soon bear you a son. You will call

him Jesus, 'one who saves,' because he will save his people from their sins." When Joseph awoke and remembered his dream, he wanted to do what the angel had said. So, the two young people soon became husband and wife.

Both Mary and Joseph were happy together as they waited for the child to be born. They wondered what sort of child this might be who was so special to God. They thought often about what the angels had said to them and also wondered to themselves if this child might be the Messiah. But they shared their thoughts with no one. They wanted only to remain quietly in Nazareth for the baby to be born.

At that time in the great city of Rome, the emperor decided that everyone in the Roman Empire should be counted. He wanted to know how many people were in his empire in order to tax them more easily. For Mary and Joseph, the population count caused a lot of trouble. Joseph was originally from Bethlehem, in Judea. Now, in order to be counted, Mary and Joseph would have to travel almost a hundred miles into the rugged hills of Judea, toward Bethlehem. They could not disobey the emperor.

Mary and Joseph soon left the green hills of Galilee behind them. The roads were full of other Jews headed for the village where they were born. With each day that Mary drew closer to the time of giving birth, Joseph grew more and more worried about her. They could not travel fast because Mary tired easily. But finally they came to Bethlehem.

The town was teeming with people. Families from all over Palestine were crowded into the small town. Joseph knew that the time for Mary to give birth had arrived. But he could not get a place in the inn. He knew, however, that an inn was not the right place for his son to be born, anyway. In those days, an inn was just one large room for many people. Mary needed quiet and privacy.

Finally, he found someone who owned a stable. Joseph led Mary there. The stable was small and full of animals, but it was warm. There was a manger there. It was usually used as a food box for the animals. But Mary would use it as a crib for the child.

That night Mary gave birth to Jesus. Joseph took him, wrapped in warm blankets, and laid him in the manger. Mary and Joseph looked quietly at their small child as he lay sleeping. They wondered, "Can this little baby, born in this simple place, the child of a simple Jewish girl, possibly be the Messiah all Israel is waiting for?" And Mary remembered the angel's words: "With God, nothing is impossible."

The hills around Bethlehem were full of shepherds with their flocks of sheep and goats. That night, a small group of shepherds watched the sheep. The sky suddenly filled with light, and an angel of God appeared. The shepherds fell to the ground, afraid.

But the angel said to them, "Do not be afraid, for I bring you good news that will cause great joy. This very night a Savior is born in Bethlehem. He is the Messiah. You can recognize this child because you will find him wrapped in blankets, lying in a manger." And then the sky filled with angels, all singing aloud, "Glory to God in the highest, and on earth peace, good will towards men."

With this song, the angels disappeared and the sky grew dark again. The only light came from the stars. The shepherds rose slowly and began to chatter about what had just happened. They could hardly believe it. They remembered the words of the angel, that they would find the child lying in a manger. Surely he would be easy to find. They went as fast as they could into Bethlehem to find him.

Soon they discovered the stable, and Mary and Joseph, and the child lying in the manger. When they saw that all the angels had said was true, they praised God in their

hearts. They told Mary and Joseph all that had happened and what the angels had said. Especially, they told Mary and Joseph the angels had called the child the Messiah.

At the word *Messiah,* Mary and Joseph and the shepherds all looked silently at the child in the manger. A little baby asleep like that was not what any of them had expected the Messiah to be. God must have special plans. The shepherds returned to the fields, praising God aloud for all they had seen and heard.

Far away to the east of Bethlehem, wise men had discovered signs of the birth of a great king. Their wisdom came from the stars. And every night they studied every star in the sky and wrote down carefully all they saw. They had discovered a new star in the sky, shining more brightly than all the others. There was much excitement.

One of the oldest wise men had studied Hebrew holy writings, and he knew the star. "It is the sign of a new king born among the Jews. Perhaps a king greater than David," he said.

They all agreed that this must be right. "Come," they said, "let us prepare. Three of us will go find this new king and worship him as we should." They prepared camels for the long journey. They collected rare presents, fit for a king: gold, frankincense, and myrrh. Gold, of course, is a rare metal. Frankincense is the sweet-smelling sap from a tree. When it burns, it gives off a spicy odor. Myrrh is also a sap, but it has a bitter odor.

Three of the wise men set out in the night, always keeping the shining star before them. The star led them to Jerusalem, where King Herod, the king of Galilee, lived. The Three Wise Men went to see Herod to find out what he knew about the newborn king. Herod sat frowning on his throne as the Wise Men spoke. "We are from the east," the Wise Men said. "We have come to see the new king of the Jews. We have seen his star. Where is he?"

Herod was worried. He was king, no one else. When he died his sons would be the next kings. He could not let someone else take his throne. But Herod was sly, for he did not tell the Wise Men his true feelings. He thought to himself, "I will get these Wise Men to find this child for me. Then, I can kill him."

Herod smiled wickedly and called for his learned men, the scribes. He asked them where the new king was supposed to be born. The Jewish scribes knew every passage in the holy writings about the Messiah. They argued among themselves for a while. Finally, one said, "According to the prophet Micah, the Messiah will be born in the small city of Bethlehem, just a few miles south of Jerusalem."

Then Herod called the Wise Men from the east to him again and said, "Go to Bethlehem. Find this child. Come

quickly back to me and tell me where he is. Then I can go and worship him myself."

So the Wise Men left Jerusalem. The star was still shining brightly in the sky. It led them to Bethlehem, and finally to the stable where Joseph, Mary, and Jesus were. The Wise Men went into the stable. When they saw the child Jesus, they knelt down together in front of him and worshipped him. Then they opened their sacks and pulled out the kingly presents they had brought from the east.

The Wise Men told Mary and Joseph how they had seen the star and traveled many days to Bethlehem to worship the new King of the Jews. Then the Wise Men spent the night with Mary and Joseph, planning to return to Herod the next day. But, while they were asleep, they were warned in a dream not to return to Herod. The next day they awoke early and returned to the east, instead, and by a different road. Herod was left waiting in Jerusalem, wondering who this new king might be and why the Wise Men had not come back. He was worried and angry.

But Mary and Joseph were safe and alone in their small stable. Mary held Jesus in her arms while he slept. The animals in the stable were quiet. Mary felt the love every mother feels when she holds her child in her arms. But Mary's thoughts kept wandering back to all the unusual things about the birth of this child. She remembered the angels who had come to her and to Joseph. The angels had said that Jesus would save Israel from its sins. She remembered the simple shepherds who had seen a sky full of angels, who had told Mary that the child was the Messiah. Then she remembered the great Wise Men from the east who had seen the star and called her new son the King of the Jews.

She looked down at little Jesus. He did not look like a king to her. But again she remembered the words of the angel: "With God, nothing is impossible."

Young Jesus

A tall soldier stood nervously outside King Herod's court. He had bad news for the king, and he was afraid of Herod's temper. He turned to a guard standing next to the main door. "What kind of mood is the king in today?" the tall soldier asked.

The guard shook his head and said, "Terrible, as always."

With that, the order came for the soldier to approach the king. Before the throne, the soldier bowed nervously.

"Well," demanded Herod, "did you find them?"

Herod would not like the answer he was about to receive. The king had been in a bad mood ever since the Wise Men had come from the east. They had told Herod that they had seen the star of a new king in Israel, a king just born. Herod had tried to trick the Wise Men into finding this child for him, so that he could kill it. But his trick had not worked. The Wise Men had never returned, as they were supposed to.

The king had waited several days and, finally, he had exploded with anger. He had ordered the soldier standing before him now to find the Wise Men and bring them in. Otherwise, it would cost the soldier his life.

The soldier had looked everywhere, but the Wise Men must have become suspicious of King Herod. They had escaped without a trace. Now, having failed in his mission, the soldier was afraid for his own life. He answered, "They have left the country. We waited too long, for they are already gone." He watched Herod closely while Herod stared back at him. The soldier knew the king was deciding whether to let him live or not.

Finally, Herod spoke. "I must find that child. I cannot let him live." Herod looked directly at the soldier. "You have failed, but I shall let you live. But I will not give up. I will find the child."

The soldier breathed a deep sigh of relief and walked quickly from the hall. Herod sat silently on his throne, thinking. He would get that child yet.

But Mary and Joseph knew nothing of Herod's plans. Their time was filled with the joy of giving their child the proper start in life. Israel was a land rich with religious traditions. When a child was born, there were many religious ceremonies that were held to celebrate the occasion.

Mary and Joseph were faithful Jews, and they followed closely all the duties of new Jewish parents. Already the child had been circumcised and named publicly in a familiar ceremony shared by every male child in Israel. Mary and Joseph's families had gathered for the special occasion. It was a time of joy.

The families had wondered about the name Jesus, which Mary and Joseph had chosen. But the two parents knew that they were obeying the commands of the angel who had appeared to them. The angel had told them to name the child Jesus, and they had.

Now Mary and Joseph were getting ready for another ceremony to be held for little Jesus. This one could be carried out only at the temple in Jerusalem.

There was an old custom among the Jews that every firstborn male child in every family belonged to the Lord. The child owed his life to service in the temple. The old custom was no longer followed, but the celebration that dedicated the firstborn to the Lord was.

There was a second reason why Mary and Joseph had to go to the temple, too. There was another Jewish custom saying that a mother was not permitted to go to public worship while she was having her baby. It was now time for Mary's welcome back into the temple. There would be a special ceremony in Jerusalem in honor of her return.

Both Mary and Joseph were excited about this special day. Eagerly, they prepared to make the trip.

In Jerusalem lived an old man named Simeon. Many years ago God had promised Simeon that he would see the Messiah before he died. For all these years Simeon had been waiting, but never had the Messiah appeared.

The old man knew that with just one glimpse he would recognize the true Messiah. Simeon had already seen many false ones. And now he was quite old and did not have much longer to live.

The day when Mary and Joseph brought the child Jesus to the temple, Simeon was there praying. He smiled to himself when he saw the couple with their child. They were obviously so happy. Simeon walked over to greet Mary and Joseph and to congratulate them on their baby.

"Good day," he said, "this is a happy day for you."

"Yes, it is," said Mary, "we are very proud."

Simeon looked with a smile at the child Jesus in his mother's arms. He caught his breath. This was the Messiah! Simeon was filled with the Spirit of God. He took the child Jesus into his arms and praised God aloud. "Lord, now You can let me die in peace. For I have seen the salvation You have prepared for all Your people."

Then, Simeon turned to Mary and spoke to her tenderly, "Your child will cause many people to fall and to rise. People will reveal the thoughts of their hearts because of him. But your own heart, Mary, will feel much pain, as if a sword was passed through it."

Mary and Joseph returned home with Jesus. They were amazed at Simeon's actions and words. What had Simeon meant? But now was the time to worry only about the baby.

Meanwhile, King Herod had not forgotten about the new child-king born in Bethlehem.

At dawn of the next day, the village quietly started to wake up. There was no hint that today would be a day of death and sorrow.

Young women gathered at the well to draw water for the day's work. The small shops on the main square were already opened. Suddenly dogs began to bark loudly at the edge of the village. The women at the well looked up. Many armed soldiers were riding hard towards the main square. But why? Soldiers never charged upon a small, peaceful town like Bethlehem unless there was dangerous business to do.

The women began to run quickly home. But it was too late. A soldier spotted one woman carrying her baby in her arms. He swerved his horse to one side of her and jerked

her child from her hands. Everyone stopped to watch. The soldier lifted the baby high over his head.

The woman shouted, "No!" and began to beat the soldier's legs with her fists. He looked at her, lowered the baby lying in his hands a little, and said, "We are only following orders. Herod has commanded that every male child two years old or younger must die. I am sorry." With that, the soldier dashed the child to the ground.

The woman ran to her child, picked up its limp, lifeless body, and cried, "You have killed my baby." She began to sob bitterly.

The rest of the soldiers charged into all the homes looking for young male children. The mothers and fathers of Bethlehem fought as best they could, but they had no swords. Some tried to hide their children, but the soldiers would always find them. Some tried to run with their children into the hills, but the soldiers on swift horses soon caught them. Everywhere, people were shouting and pleading. But everywhere, soldiers were doing their terrible job.

Finally the killing was done. Bethehem was filled with loud crying and shouting. No one had ever dreamed such a horrible thing would happen. Even the soldiers stood silently and sadly in the square.

A young father who had lost his son fell on his knees before the soldiers. Then he cried aloud to them, "Cursed be your King Herod. Someday he will pay for this. God will bring justice to this land. He will send us the Messiah to rid us of evil kings."

The captain of the soldiers ordered his men to mount their horses. They rode out of town with the tears and curses of the Jews sounding in their ears. The captain turned to a soldier at his side. "This is a miserable job we have to do. I wish I were not a soldier today. I will never forget this terrible day."

The other soldier nodded his head and added, "Herod is a cruel man."

King Herod sat brooding on his throne. He was used to killing people. He had even put his own sons to death for rebelling against him. But today he felt uneasy. He was still worried.

Herod did not dare to let a king live, one that might become a rival. This is why he had decided to kill every young male child in the area around Bethlehem. He knew that it was an awful thing to do, but he had to get rid of the new king in order to protect the throne. Herod loved his power more than anything else in the world.

But even with all the little boys dead, Herod was still not satisfied. Suppose that, for all the slaughter, he had not gotten the right child? Perhaps this new king had somehow escaped and would one day return to take Herod's throne away from him and his family. Herod was so worried, he was not able to sleep.

Where was Jesus? The little baby was with his parents, on the main road south of Jerusalem, the one that went down to Egypt. Joseph and Mary were leading a donkey with all they owned on its back. Safely in her arms, Mary held the child. She was telling Joseph that she did not want to go to Egypt.

Joseph explained to her again. "Mary, we must do what the angel told me last night while I was sleeping. When the angel appeared to me in my dream, he said Herod would try to kill Jesus and that we must go to Egypt. Don't worry. We will be all right. It is God's will."

But Mary replied, "We have no family in Egypt, Joseph. Everyone we know lives either in Bethlehem or Nazareth. It is hard for me to leave our family and friends behind."

"Yes," Joseph agreed. "But remember that Egypt is a rich land. Many Jews live there, too. I can find work easily, and we can make friends among the other Jews. You'll see.

Even in Egypt we can find people who share our belief in God. It will be a good life."

Mary was quiet. God seemed to be taking special care of the child in her arms.

Life in Egypt was good for Mary and Joseph, but they missed home the whole time they were there. They could not go home as long as King Herod still lived. Then, one night, Joseph had another dream. Once again an angel appeared to him, saying, "Get up and take Mary and the child back home to Nazareth. The one who has been trying to kill Jesus is no more." The evil King Herod had finally died.

Immediately Mary and Joseph took the young Jesus and returned home to Israel. When they came to the area around Bethlehem, they learned that Herod's son, who now ruled, was living near there. They were afraid of him, so they decided to go farther north to little Nazareth.

Nazareth was located in a beautiful area called Galilee, a fine place in Palestine to raise a family. Its hills were soft and green, not like the rough brown hills near Bethlehem. The rich land provided all the towns with plenty of food. To the east was the Sea of Galilee. It was full of fish. Those who caught the fish sent them throughout Galilee to all the small towns, including Nazareth. No one would ever starve in Galilee.

Nazareth itself was nestled in the small hills to the south. It looked out over a rich valley. Joseph found plenty of work as a carpenter there. And Nazareth had a fine synagogue where Joseph could take his family for worship every Sabbath.

As Jesus grew older, he loved especially to go to the synagogue, where holy writings would be read aloud to the people, and learned scribes, or scholars, would explain their meaning. And here in Nazareth Jesus began to grow not only in height but also in wisdom.

Every year Mary, Joseph, and Jesus would go up to Jerusalem for the Passover celebration. The Passover was the main religious celebration of the year for the Jews. Entire families from all over Galilee, Judea, and neighboring areas would travel to Jerusalem for this serious but happy occasion.

It was a time of great excitement for young Jesus. Jerusalem teemed with people. He met youngsters from other parts of the world. He saw the magnificent temple King Herod had built. He listened to all the great Jewish wise men who would take this chance to teach the people about the traditions of their forefathers.

When Jesus was twelve years old, his family, as usual, went to Jerusalem for the Passover. When the celebration was over, Mary and Joseph could not find Jesus anywhere in the crowd. After Joseph had looked for him for quite some time, he said to Mary, "Come, let us return home. Jesus is a smart young boy. I am certain that he is with some of our friends. Let's let him travel with them today, and we will find him tonight—after we stop."

But that night they could not find Jesus. They went to all the families of Nazareth. They asked all their relatives, but no one had seen Jesus.

Mary and Joseph returned to Jerusalem. At first, they could not find their son. Then, after three days, there he was—sitting in the temple. He was talking with the wise men of Jerusalem, listening to them and asking them questions. Every one of them was amazed at the child's wisdom. How could a boy so young be so wise about God?

Then Jesus said to Mary, "Why were you looking for me? Do you not know that I should be here in my Father's house?" But Mary and Joseph did not understand.

Jesus obeyed Mary and Joseph and went back with them, back to Nazareth. It was not until many years later that Jesus would again teach in the temple.

John, preacher in the wilderness

John the Baptist was a rough and powerful man. He wore camel's hair for clothes and tied a leather belt around his waist. For food he ate wild grasshoppers and honey. He did not like cities. John the Baptist felt that cities made the people soft and lazy. He preferred the rough wilderness of Judea.

And this is where he lived with his followers—on the rocky hills, under the hot sun. A hard life makes a person strong. And John the Baptist was a strong man.

Many Jews loved the wilderness, so John was not alone. For years women and men had roamed the hills around the Dead Sea and the valleys near the Jordan River. They were escaping from the cities, which they felt were full of temptation and sin. In Jerusalem, for example, it was hard to be a good Jew. There were so many temptations. But here in the wilderness the hard life meant hard work, too. There was little time to fall into sinful habits.

One day John was standing on the rocky ground next to the Jordan River. Gathered around him were all sorts of men and women, from all over Israel. Some were rich. Some were poor. Many loved John and thought that God had sent him. There were also many who had come only to stare at this man they had heard was so strange and dressed so unusually. And many had come to make fun of John, who sometimes acted almost as if he was crazy.

"Hello, you sinners." John's voice was loud and angry as he shouted at the crowd around him. "What brings you out here away from your soft life?

"I tell you that every Jew who does not repent today, confessing all sins, will not be saved. I don't care if you are the grandson of David himself. Unless you do good deeds, you will burn in hell. I warn you, repent, for the Kingdom of God is at hand."

John had many followers. They had left their homes and now lived with him in this hard wilderness. Their life was one of prayer and fasting: day after day, John and his followers would eat no food. Instead, they would spend their time only talking and praying.

The followers loved to hear John talk. His voice seemed to grow louder and louder: "Listen to me. I tell you the end of the world is coming soon. God will destroy all the sinful cities in which you live. And God will judge everyone. You must repent and start doing good deeds right now."

An old Pharisee, a religious leader, from Jerusalem sat in the hot sun listening to these angry words from John. The Pharisee had heard there was a strange person making predictions in the wilderness, and the old man had come to see the prophet.

The Pharisees in Jerusalem had seen many men like John come and go. They knew the wilderness was full of false prophets, just as it was full of false messiahs. Many times in the last few years, Jews had gathered in this wilderness around one of these so-called messengers of God. The prophet had convinced the listeners that the world was coming to an end and that the Messiah was coming to save Israel. But the Messiah had not come. The prophets had all been wrong.

"This John seems like all the other false teachers," the Pharisee thought. "He is only misleading the people. God will judge us, but only when we die. You cannot find God by yourself in the wilderness. You can find the will of God only in the holy writings and in tradition."

But the Pharisee said nothing about his opinions to John.

He just sat quietly, wondering why so many people were following the strange man.

John's voice was still strong: "Don't think that being a Jew is enough to save you. Don't say to yourself, 'Abraham is my forefather, so God will save me.' This very day, the ax is cutting down the trees. And every bad tree will be thrown into the fire."

The crowd grew nervous and loud. People began to shout at John.

"What can we do?"

"We want to be saved."

"Share everything that you have," answered John. "If you have two coats and you meet someone who has none, then give up one of yours. If you have food, and you meet someone who has none, share yours."

Suddenly from the midst of the crowd a loud voice shouted out, "What about me?"

It was the voice of a tax collector. Every Jew in Israel hated the tax collectors. They were worse than the Romans themselves, for they were Jews who worked for the Romans. And the tax collectors cheated. If a Jew owed five pieces of silver in taxes, the tax collector might take ten pieces and keep the extra five for himself.

John knew who the man was and said, "You, too, must repent, but also you must never cheat again."

The prophet had not spoken roughly to the tax collector. A soldier standing nearby heard the reasonable words and gained the courage to speak out himself.

"What about me?" he cried.

John knew that soldiers cheated, too. A soldier's pay was small, and nearly every soldier would take money by force when he needed it.

John said, "Be satisfied with your wages. Never steal from anyone."

John's words had not been rough either to the tax collector or to the soldier. The old Pharisee had listened carefully. He wondered if maybe John was different from all the other prophets he had seen.

The Pharisee, curious, raised his voice and cried out, "What about me?"

John looked hard at the old Pharisee, then said, "You Pharisees are all like snakes. What makes you think you can escape God's judgment? You must do good deeds and then you must repent."

The Pharisee was quiet. John's words had been hard. But John still seemed different from the other false prophets because his answer to the questions was simply to do good deeds. The Pharisee had to agree that doing good deeds was what God wanted.

Then a young man stood up in the crowd and laughed at John. "You know, you are crazy. You think dressing in weird clothes and living in the wilderness will save you? I don't think you act like a prophet. To me it seems you act like a man who has a demon inside him. If you ask me, I think you are just a crazy fool."

Other voices began to ring out:

"No, he is the Messiah."

"No, not the Messiah, but he is a great prophet. Maybe he is Elijah reborn."

Then many voices cried out together, "John, are you the Messiah?"

"No, I am not the Messiah," answered John. "But I promise you that there is one coming after me who is much stronger than I am."

Then John walked down from the rocks to the edge of the river. He pointed at the water flowing by and said, "I will baptize you with water, but I am only the forerunner. The one who comes after me will baptize you with the Holy Spirit and with fire."

John waded out into the flowing water. "Come," he

said. "If the end is near, now is the time to be baptized. Repent, and this water will clean you of all your sins."

Many people in the crowd believed John. They waded out into the water, into the Jordan River, with him. One by one they came to him. They confessed their sins to God. They promised to do good deeds from then on. Then John grabbed them and dunked them into the water.

All the time John was baptizing he continued shouting to the crowd: "Repent, repent, for the Kingdom of God is at hand."

But suddenly John stopped shouting. He saw a man coming towards him who was not like the others. No one but John recognized him. This man was Jesus.

And John said very quietly, "Why have you come to me to be baptized? It is you who should baptize me."

But Jesus answered him, saying, "For today it is best that I am baptized by you."

John took Jesus and baptized him in the Jordan River. And all this time the followers of John watched. And the old Pharisee watched, too. They had never seen John so quiet. They wondered who the other man in the water might be.

When Jesus came up out of the water, it looked as though the heavens opened up. A white dove came down from the sky to where Jesus stood.

Then, all who were at the river heard a voice from the heavens say, "This is My beloved Son, in whom I am well pleased."

John's followers came to him and asked, "Who is that man?"

And John said, "He is the Lamb of God."

From that day, many of John's followers left him and began to follow Jesus.

The old Pharisee from Jerusalem did not know what to think. He stayed for much of the day, listening to John. He had heard many unusual things, including voices from heaven. The Pharisee had to admit that John was not like all the other prophets.

The old man knew that many people hated the Pharisees. He also knew that many people had fled from the cities to live in the wilderness. On the edge of the Dead Sea, there was an entire community who lived together to get away from city life.

This community also hated the Pharisees and all the priests in Jerusalem. They had called the temple in Jerusalem dirty and worthless. Like John, they thought the end of the world was coming soon. They were certain that the Messiah, the Son of God, would come and lead a great army against all the enemies of Israel.

They waited eagerly for that day to come. Like John, they baptized themselves to keep clean from sin.

The old Pharisee thought about all the false messiahs who had misled the people. There had been many of them. Some were killed by soldiers, and some simply disappeared. There had been so many false prophets that most of the Pharisees thought that God had stopped sending real prophets at all.

The Pharisees felt that if there were no more real prophets, then the only way to find out what God wanted you to do was to study the holy writings. So, the Pharisees did not go out into the wilderness to find God. Instead, they studied the holy writings and all the sayings of the great wise men of Israel.

"Surely," the old Pharisee thought as he walked home, "we are doing the right thing. Surely God is to be found in study and in tradition, not in eating grasshoppers outside in the wilderness."

Still, it was hard to forget about John.

When an old Pharisee knew the holy writings well, it was not unusual for him to try to recall passages from the writings that explained the world around him. That is what the old man was doing as night fell and he continued home. He kept thinking about a passage from the Book of Isaiah, the prophet. It was a saying about the dawning of the Kingdom of God. The words were:

"A voice is crying in the wilderness, 'Prepare the way of the Lord. Make His paths straight.' "

But the Pharisee shook his head. "No," he thought. "This man John is not a sign of the coming of the Kingdom of God. No. Perhaps he is better than the other false prophets, but, still, he is just misleading the people.

"The Messiah will not come soon. As for John himself, he probably will not live long. Already he is causing too much trouble. Soon the king will grow tired of him and will have him killed.

"Yes, John will be killed."

John dies a prisoner

John the Baptist knew his life was in danger. He looked out over the heads of the large throng of people in front of him. They were from all over Palestine, and they had gathered to hear him preach.

The crowd was stirring with excitement. Some were listening to this rough prophet for the first time. But many had been following him for quite a while. John was strange and striking in his camel's hair clothes. The people leaned forward, fascinated as he began shouting. He said that the world was coming to an end.

"Maybe he's the Messiah," said one of the crowd.

"No," said another. "But he says that the Messiah is going to come soon."

"Yes, and we will finally be rid of these foreigners—these Romans—who rule us."

"There will be a great war, and maybe the angels of God will fight at our side. And the Romans go for good."

The noise from the crowd became almost deafening. The people set up a shout that became louder and louder. Large groups came forward to John to be baptized. The prophet noticed that this crowd was even larger than yesterday's. More people were coming to him every day.

Standing on a hill a short distance away, there were two soldiers. They were in the service of King Herod Antipas. Herod ruled Galilee and the land lying just east of the Jordan River.

The soldiers were nervous because the crowd seemed to be getting out of hand. "Come on," said one, "let's get out of here. This man John is too dangerous. I think we'd better warn King Herod. You know, I think he is too soft on John the Baptist. Herod should have done away with him a long time ago. Don't you agree?"

The other soldier answered, "Herod is afraid that the people will revolt if he arrests John. But, if something is not done soon, these people here today will turn on the soldiers—on us. Then the killing will begin."

"These Jews are crazy," the first soldier replied. "They are always following some messiah who claims he will conquer Rome. It's laughable. They cannot conquer Rome.

"Every time one of these messiahs gets out of hand, we simply have to ride in with our swords and kill him and all his followers. And then things settle down for a while. I wish Herod would just give us the go ahead."

"Well, I agree that it's time Herod sent us to take care of this John the Baptist. Come on. Let's go tell Herod what we have seen here today."

Herod Antipas was the son of the evil King Herod the Great. But Herod Antipas himself was not an evil man. He did have two problems: one was John the Baptist and his dangerous followers. The other was Herodias, Herod Antipas' wife.

Actually, his problems had begun because of Herodias. Herod fell in love with her when he was already married to the daughter of the powerful king of the Nabateans, a strong desert tribe to the south. Herodias was already married, too. She was the wife of Herod's own half brother. But Herod loved her, so he divorced his first wife to marry Herodias.

Because of this marriage, Herod now had two powerful enemies. The King of the Nabateans hated him for divorcing his daughter. And John the Baptist condemned him for marrying his own brother's wife. Herod did not know what to do.

When Herod heard the report of his two soldiers, his wife Herodias was sitting at his side. She seethed with anger at every word the soldiers said. She hated John the Baptist. After the soldiers left, Herodias said to Herod, "You must kill John. He is too dangerous."

"I cannot kill him," answered Herod. "The people think he is a great prophet. If I kill him, they will surely revolt. And I must remember the Romans. They do not like revolutions. If there is trouble, they will take away my throne."

"Yes," Herodias answered carefully. She knew she must be clever to convince her husband. "You must remember the Romans. But tell me something. What will the Romans do if John leads his disciples in revolt, after you have done nothing to stop him?"

Herod shifted nervously in his chair. Herodias saw that she was making progress, so she continued.

"John is making a fool of you. Day after day he tells the people it was wrong for you to marry me. He says many evil things about me, too. If you loved me, you would not put up with him. You must kill him. You must."

Herod sat quietly thinking. Finally, he turned to his wife and said, "No, I shall not kill John the Baptist. Not even for you. But I will shut him up for a while."

"Guards!" commanded Herod. Two guards entered immediately. "Arrest John the Baptist."

It was not long before John sat alone in a dark cell. The soldiers had arrested him without telling him his crime. But John knew why he was in prison. It was because he had spoken out against Herod's wife. John also knew that he would probably never get out of the prison. Herod had put him in one of the strongest fortresses in the land. That meant Herod feared John and his disciples, his followers, too much ever to let him go.

One day, several weeks after John had been arrested, he heard a clanging at the cell door. There were voices outside. Then the door swung open and two men walked in. These were two of John's disciples.

"Master," one of them said, "are you all right?"

"Yes, I am fine," replied John. "Tell me, how are my people? What is happening outside?"

"Master, there is news of Jesus. Many of your people are with him now. When Jesus heard you were in prison, he came into Galilee and began to preach. We hear wonderful stories of miracles, that he is healing the sick."

"Yes, Master," the second disciple said, "it's true. I myself have heard him teach. He speaks with strength and wisdom. Some people think he is the Messiah."

John listened carefully. Then he leaned forward and spoke quietly to his disciples. There was excitement in his voice. "Yes, I know Jesus. I remember the day I baptized him. I wondered even then if he might be the one we are waiting for. Listen, you must go and follow him. Ask him if he is the Messiah. Then, quickly, come tell me what you have learned."

The disciples hurried out. John sat alone again in his cell. He wondered, "Can Jesus be the one? I must know soon, for I am afraid I haven't long to live."

At the end of a long day, Jesus withdrew from the crowd to be alone with his disciples. The two men sent by John had joined the group, following Jesus all day long. They had seen and heard many things, and now they came forward to speak to Jesus in order to ask him John's question: Was he the Messiah?

Jesus turned towards them as they approached. "Master," they said, "we are from John, who is in prison. He has heard of the wonderful things you do. He wants to know if you are the one we are waiting for. Or, should we wait for another?"

Jesus answered, "Tell John what you have heard and seen as you followed me. The blind can see again, and the lame can now walk. Lepers are cleansed, and the deaf hear. The dead are raised up, and the poor have good news preached to them."

With this message, the two disciples returned to John, still in his cell. When John heard the words, he understood them. He remembered the great prophet Isaiah, who said that when the Messiah came, the blind would see, the lame would walk, and the poor would be comforted. John understood, but he also knew that he would never see Jesus again. Herodias, the king's wife, would never let John out of prison alive.

One day, as John lingered in his cell, Herodias dressed up in her finest clothes. It was Herod's birthday. All the officers of Herod's court and all the rich men in Galilee were to gather for a feast.

Herod was happy and full of fun when the party began. His thoughts were far away from the troubles of his kingdom. He thought only of having a good time, of being a good host, and of watching the entertainment.

Herod leaned back contentedly to watch the show. He sighed with satisfaction. There were some days he loved being a ruler. He sat up slightly when he saw a young dancing girl enter the room. He loved dancers.

He watched her closely as she glided without effort across the floor. He knew this girl. Yes, it was his wife Herodias' daughter, his step-daughter. Many times he had seen her and admired her beauty. She danced magnificently. Herod could not take his eyes off her.

"Beautiful," Herod said, "just beautiful."

When she finished her dance, Herod said, "Young girl, I must give you a present. Never have I enjoyed a dance so much. I swear to you that I will give you anything you ask for, even half my kingdom."

The young girl did not know what to say. She suddenly turned and ran out of the room. She went to her mother.

Herodias listened to her daughter's story and smiled. This was her chance. "I will tell you what to ask for," Herodias said. "You must ask for the head of John the Baptist on a platter."

Her daughter ran back into the room and announced, "Give me the head of John the Baptist on a platter."

Herod could not believe his ears. She wanted John's head? Herod knew there was no way out. He had sworn to give her whatever she wanted. He had to keep his word.

So, Herod had John the Baptist executed. John's head was brought on a platter and given to the girl. She took it to her mother. Herodias held up John's head by his hair and smiled at her victory.

John's disciples buried John's body and came to tell Jesus what had happened. And Jesus stood up before a crowd and spoke to them about John. "Why did you go out into the wilderness to see John?" he asked. "Did you go to see a man dressed in fine clothes? No, for you can see men dressed in fine clothes in the houses of kings.

"Did you go out to see a great prophet? I tell you that John is greater than all the prophets. There is no one greater than John. He is the one who has prepared the way for the Messiah.

"But you did not really accept him, did you? And you do not really accept me, either. You thought John was crazy because he dressed in rough clothes and followed all the laws of Israel. And you think I am a sinner because I eat with sinners and tax collectors."

Then Jesus and his disciples withdrew to a lonely place.

As for Herod, the future held sadness. Years after John the Baptist's death, the king of the Nabateans made war against Herod and defeated him. Herod lost his kingdom. And, all over Palestine, people said, "God has now punished Herod for killing John the Baptist."

Jesus triumphs over Satan

Alone, Jesus waited in the wilderness. Hot and dust-covered and tired, he stood on the rocky ground, studying the horizon. Jesus was waiting for an enemy to appear—a powerful opponent who was coming to test the Son of God.

Some people might think that Jesus' enemy was Rome, the empire that ruled the Jews with laws that seemed at times too harsh to bear. The soldiers stopped at nothing to make Rome's power felt. But neither Rome nor its soldiers were the enemy Jesus waited for.

The burning wind blew across the barren earth. Jesus felt the scorching sun of the wilderness beating down on his bare head. His body was weak from hunger. But he would not hide himself from his enemy. Jesus quietly stood there, waiting for his foe to appear.

Some people might suppose that Jesus' enemy were the Pharisees and the other religious leaders of the Jews. These leaders soon would look upon Jesus as just another false—but dangerous—messiah. Already they had singled out John the Baptist, Jesus' forerunner, for their suspicion. The religious leaders would not put up with anyone who wished to turn the people away from the traditional ways of worshipping God.

But the Pharisees were not the enemy Jesus waited for. His eyes searched the hardness of the desert for someone else, someone who should be approaching now and would soon reach him.

The young Jew had been praying all by himself for many

days. The prayers had made his soul strong. He was ready for the enemy's test. Forty days ago John had baptized Jesus in the River Jordan. At that moment, Jesus had been filled with the Spirit of God. It was this spirit that had led Jesus into the wilderness, where he now stood.

For forty days and forty nights, Jesus had been alone in this desert. All this time, he had eaten nothing. Before him lay his work, his ministry. He would soon return to the cities of Galilee and Judea. There, he would teach and heal many people.

But, first, Jesus had to face his enemy.

Then, who was it? Could Jesus have been waiting for the people themselves? Jesus knew that soldiers would nail him to a cross and leave him there to suffer until death. There would be only a few sorrowing people at the foot of the cross. One would be his mother Mary. Would any others reach out their hands to help him? No, they would not. The people—even his best friends—would abandon Jesus in the final agony of Calvary, the place where his cross would stand. But the people were not Jesus' enemy today.

Jesus gave a start. The time had come. His opponent had appeared. It was an expert in wickedness, an evil spirit, coming to test Jesus. The enemy was Satan himself.

Satan had followed humankind all through time. Where was it that he lurked? Perhaps he was with Cain when, in a fit of jealousy, he slew his brother Abel. Perhaps he was in Goliath's smile as the Philistine giant planned to kill the shepherd boy David. We know Satan was with Job, tormenting him with tragedy and disease until the weakened man cried out to the God he loved, asking the reason for his suffering.

And now Satan was with Jesus, the Son of God.

He looked carefully at Jesus' tired body and saw the hunger there. Satan bent over, lifting a stone from the hot earth. Grinning, he began the test: "You look terribly hungry, Jesus. If you are the Son of God, then turn this stone into bread. Surely the Son of God can do that."

But Jesus was ready to do battle with Satan. He would not use weapons or harsh words. Satan was an expert in violence and evil speaking. Jesus, instead, would protect himself with his faith in God and his knowledge of the holy writings of his people.

Jesus answered Satan in this way: "The holy writings say that people will not live by bread alone. They will live instead by every word that comes from the mouth of God. I do not have to turn stones into bread so that I can have food. My food comes from God."

Satan frowned. Jesus would not be an easy opponent. Even hunger, it seemed, had not weakened his faith. Satan had understood the answer. It meant that God would support Jesus always and in every way. Mere food could not support people as God could. "So, God will support Jesus," Satan thought to himself. "We will have to see about that." He decided to take a different approach. He needed a special strategy for this special opponent.

The city of Jerusalem was familiar to Satan, especially the holy places there. Sometimes these were the best places for him to tempt people into turning away from God. He had seen people make a show of being holy many times at the temple. Sometimes they would brag about giving money to the poor, when they really had given the money only to make themselves look good in front of their friends. Sometimes the people at the temple whipped and beat others in the name of holiness. They would even kill, right near the temple, stoning people accused of crimes.

"Yes," Satan thought to himself, "I will take Jesus to the temple. That is the best place to test him again."

When they arrived in Jerusalem, Satan took Jesus to the highest tower of the temple. "Look down," Satan said, "down to the street below. It's a long drop, isn't it?" Jesus looked down, saying nothing.

"Why not show me you are the Son of God, Jesus, since that is what you claim? The Son of God is so powerful, he could never die, right? Even if he fell off the highest tower of this temple. Well, show me, Jesus. Throw yourself down and prove to me that the fall will not kill you."

Jesus looked thoughtfully at Satan, but still said nothing. Then Satan had a new idea. He smiled wickedly. Jesus had quoted the holy writings earlier, when he had refused to turn the stone into bread. Satan was an expert in the holy writings, too. He knew them and could use them to his advantage.

Satan said, "Jesus, are you worried about tossing yourself off this tower? Remember, the holy writings say that if you are the Son of God, the angels will take care of you. I have read that they will hold you up in their own hands. They will not even let you stub your foot on a stone.

"Why do you hesitate now to leap off this tower? Do you doubt the power of the angels, the angels of the Lord?"

Now Jesus answered simply: "Satan, it is not our place to test God. I will not tempt the Lord just because you want me to."

Again, Satan frowned. Jesus was proving much harder to argue with than Satan had expected. Weakened and hungry, Jesus was still mindful of his respect for the Lord.

But Satan had one final temptation in mind for Jesus. All the Jews, Satan knew, were waiting eagerly for their Messiah. They wanted him to be a powerful king who ruled over a powerful nation. They longed for their own Jewish king—a king sent by God, a king who would replace the Romans and rule with justice.

Satan knew of a high mountain where he now led Jesus. From the very top, he and Jesus could see all the shining kingdoms of the earth. There was glory and wealth in their cities. Even King Solomon, once known for his wisdom, had turned greedy because of his love for riches. Perhaps Satan could tempt Jesus with the same prize. Jesus might turn from God in exchange for all this dazzling wealth.

Satan stretched out his hand, pointing to the cities of luxury, the jewels of the earth. Jerusalem was one. And there was also powerful Rome. Both cities glittered in the sunlight. Jesus and Satan could also see Alexandria, in Egypt. This beautiful port city beside the Nile River held vast libraries and a great university. And then there was Athens, in Greece. Its white marble temples reflected pure white against the beautiful Mediterranean sky. Surely, thought Satan, there must be something in every one of these cities that would tempt Jesus away from God.

And now Satan spoke this way to Jesus: "Do you see all these kingdoms? Jesus, I can give you every one if you will just fall down and worship me."

Jesus looked away from the kingdoms of the world. He had not seen glory and wealth in what Satan could give him. The kingdoms held many wonders, that was true. But there was no land on earth that Jesus wanted. The kingdom he sought was the Kingdom of God.

"Get away from me, Satan. Get behind me for good," Jesus commanded. "The holy writings say that all the people of the earth will worship the Lord God and only Him. I, too, will worship only God. It is the kingdom He has to offer that has value for me, not any kingdom you could show me. Go away from me. Begone!"

Again, Jesus stood alone. The temptation was over. With faith in the Lord, Jesus had defeated Satan, his enemy.

Jesus knew that the Kingdom of God was not going to be like the great lands he had seen from the mountaintop. Jesus had come to serve the people, not to be served by them. He would not wear a golden crown and have many people to wait on him.

In the future stood a cross, one on which Jesus would die. The people would see his power in that cross, not from a mighty throne. The people would not remember Jesus giving great celebrations in a great court, dressed in kingly robes. They would remember his suffering.

They would see him wearing a dirt-spattered robe with red slashes across the back—bloody slashes that had been made by the whips of Roman soldiers. Jesus' crown would be one of thorns that dug into his forehead and pierced his skin. His wrists would not be decorated with fine bracelets. Instead, they would be scarred with the marks of nails, nails driven into his flesh to hang him from the cross.

Jesus knew that many people would not understand why he had chosen the Kingdom of God over the kingdom of man, the kingdom Satan had offered him. He also knew that Satan would not give up. He would come again to test the Son of God. He would be with Jesus in the Garden of Gethsemane, where Jesus would tremble as he awaited the Roman soldiers. And Satan would be with Jesus in his final moments on the cross. Then, Jesus would cry out to his Father, asking why the Lord God had forsaken him. The temptation would not really end until Jesus had died and risen again from the grave.

Straightening his tired shoulders, Jesus looked sadly into the wilderness that faced him. It was now time to go back to the hillsides, where the people waited for him to speak. It was time also to go back to the cities, where the temples needed his guidance.

Jesus would see his enemy Satan again, but in a different place. Now, it was time for Jesus to go back, to begin the work of God.

Cana: Jesus' first miracle

Jesus first began teaching along the shores of the Sea of Galilee. There, the breeze was warm and fragrant and the water glistened in the sun.

The Sea of Galilee is not a salt sea. It is really a small, freshwater lake. Many fish live in the Sea of Galilee. Except in one spot where the flat plain of Gennesaret cuts through, gentle, sloping hills lie along its shores. It is on these hills where crowds gathered to hear and see Jesus, the teacher from Nazareth. In the southern hills, the people could pick the figs, olives, dates, and pomegranates that grew wild there. This fruit would take away the bite of hunger as the day grew longer and the followers remained to listen to the new teacher.

More and more people came as word spread and Jesus' popularity grew. News traveled before him and, wherever he went along the sea, people came to hear him.

But the people had been listening to messiahs for quite some time. Just because Jesus was a popular teacher today did not necessarily mean that the people thought he was the Son of God, the true Messiah. It could have meant only that the people who crowded around him found his words comforting and kind. Or perhaps the crowds simply found him more interesting than other teachers.

After Jesus had gathered his disciples around him, he left the shores of the Sea of Galilee and walked up to the hills. He was going to a wedding in a town named Cana. There, he would do what no ordinary man could do. He would perform a miracle. And, as news of his miracle spread to the people, they would begin to believe more and more that Jesus was the Messiah.

Jesus and his disciples walked towards Cana, west of the sea. They climbed hills full of olive trees, and they passed fields of grain, rows of vineyards, and small farms. The vineyards grew dark, juice-filled, sweet-smelling grapes for the wine that was used on feast days and special celebrations. The wedding day was one of the important days when wine was served. Jesus and his disciples knew that, if all went according to custom, the guests at the wedding at Cana would drink wine to toast the bride and the groom.

Jesus and his disciples traveled slowly because crowds gathered to walk and talk with Jesus and to hear what he said. It took three days to reach Cana. When the group at last arrived, Jesus' mother Mary was already there.

Mary had probably arrived at Cana for the very beginning of the wedding celebration. This was when the bride and groom walked through the streets of the town. Following them would be their guests, who sang songs, tossed flowers, and danced as the procession made its way through the streets.

In the time of Jesus, weddings sometimes lasted as long as a week. Guests came and went, always toasting the groom and bride. They would sing and dance to the music of cymbals, clarinets, tambourines, and harps. Also, the families of the young couple would serve many special and delicious foods besides the rich wine that came from the vineyards.

One important person at the wedding was called the "governor of the feast." He made sure that the servants kept the tables full of food. He also sampled the wine before it was poured for the guests, testing the wine for taste.

The bride and the groom were sitting together at a table when Jesus arrived. Veils and crowns of flowers covered their heads. Jewelry adorned their fingers, wrists, ankles, necks—even their noses.

Also at the table with the groom and bride were some guests. Servants brought them fish and lamb, barley and wheat breads, boiled and dried locusts, dates, raisins, pomegranates, olives, cheeses, honey cakes, and wine. Everyone ate hungrily from the dishes of rich food. But from their goblets, the guests did not drink, for the wine had run out. There was no more.

In the courtyard, there were six large waterpots. The water in them was not used for drinking, though. It was used for washing. At the doorway, a young servant waited for the guests to arrive. When they did, the servant would take water from one of the pots and wash the dust from the guests' hands and feet.

When Jesus arrived, Mary, seeing her son, came to greet him, saying, "It is a shame, but they have already run out of wine for the wedding."

Jesus looked at his mother and understood that she wanted him to solve the problem. He told her, "Mother, I can do nothing about the wine. The time has not quite come when I shall begin my work. It is not yet time for me to show the world who I am."

But Jesus' mother believed he would do something. He knew the importance of wine to the guests and to the bridegroom, who was the host of the wedding.

Mary went to the servants and told them, "When my son asks, be sure to do whatever he says." Mary seemed to know that the moment had come when Jesus would begin to perform his miracles.

Jesus called the servants to him. "Fill the waterpots in the courtyard to the brim," he said.

After they had done so, Jesus gave them the next instructions: "Now, take some water from the pots," he said, "and serve it to the governor of the feast."

The servants did as Jesus said. They took water from the pots and, going to the governor, said, "Would you please taste this wine?"

The governor of the feast took the liquid and looked at it. It looked like wine. Then he sniffed it and twirled it in its bowl. The fragrance of wine drifted up to his nostrils. Then he brought the bowl to his lips, first taking a tiny lap with his tongue. He smiled and took a hearty swallow.

"Why, this is excellent wine," the governor said, surprised. "A wine of the highest quality."

Where had the wine come from? The governor did not know. But the servants who had brought him the wine knew. It had come from the waterpots.

Next, the governor of the feast told the bridegroom about the wine. "That was a good thing for you to do," said the governor. "Most people give their guests the best wine at the beginning of the feast. Then, after the guests have sipped quite a bit of it and won't notice, the bridegroom serves the wine that is not as good.

"I see now that you kept the best wine for last, for near the end of the wedding feast." Soon, the wine was served all around.

The disciples who had followed Jesus from the Sea of Galilee had seen Jesus turn the water into wine. They wondered at the miracle. There had been many men who had called themselves messiahs. But none of the disciples had ever heard of one who had been able to turn ordinary water into wine.

And the guests at the wedding also learned of the miracle. Word began to spread.

One man said, "I suspected that we would see no more wine. Now the bridegroom is serving better wine than he did at the beginning of the feast."

"Yes," another replied, "and I hear that the wine was sitting in the waterpots all this time."

"No, you're wrong," a third said. "I just came into the courtyard. The servant washed my feet with water from one of those pots. I think there was water in all the other pots when I came in, too."

The third man's wife nudged him. "I know this is unbelievable, but that guest over there, Mary's son, Jesus of Nazareth? One of the fellows who came in with him told me that it was Jesus who turned the water into wine."

The word about Jesus spread this way, from guest to guest. Finally, the news made its way into the town of Cana, too, and then throughout the countryside. Even more people became curious about Jesus, wanting to see him and hear what he had to say.

In this way Jesus performed his first miracle at a wedding in the town of Cana, high in the hills of the Sea of Galilee. Many more miracles were to follow soon.

Because he loved: Jesus' miracles

"It's getting late, Peter," Andrew told his brother. "The sun will soon be going down behind the hills. Look at all the people who have come to hear Jesus speak. There must be five thousand of them. What will they eat for dinner?"

Leaning back against a cypress tree, Peter shifted his strong, muscular body into a more comfortable position. His hands, with nails cracked and skin scarred from years of fishing, brushed against the tree. The fisherman turned his face, bold as an eagle's, to look at the crowds.

"They will never leave for their homes as long as they have hope that Jesus will heal or comfort them," Peter said. "You know how many miracles he has performed. Everyone is talking about them."

With worried eyes, Peter looked at his master standing before the crowd. Jesus had been with the people all day. He should have been as weary as the drooping white petals of the lilies climbing the low hills around the sea. Yet, Jesus still had a quiet strength—just like the tall cypress tree Peter leaned against.

Andrew said to Peter, "Have you ever sat back and tried to count all the wonderful things Jesus has done in such a short time?"

"Oh, yes," replied Peter. "And do you remember how the crowds first treated Jesus? They were so afraid of his power, they begged him to leave, to go away."

Andrew shook his head. "Yes. That happened when he cured the crazy man in the graveyard. I'll never forget how that pitiful fellow looked when we first saw him. Re-

member? We had just pulled our boat ashore when he came running and yelling toward us. Broken chains hung from his wrists. No one was able to make anything strong enough to hold him. His clothes were bloody and torn where he had cut himself with sharp stones. He was a real lunatic, poor man."

Peter added, "And his screams—remember that sound? The bravest person would tremble to hear those shrieks. When he fell down at Jesus' feet, I thought the lunatic was dead. But Jesus spoke to the unclean spirits inside and ordered them out so that the man could be sane again."

"What amazed me," Andrew continued, "was how the unclean spirits left the man and went into the bodies of the pigs feeding on the hillside. I was shocked when the swine turned and raced in a panic, right over the cliff into the sea. That was when the people came out of the nearby towns and begged Jesus to go away and leave them alone. They were so frightened by the miracle, they asked Jesus to leave."

Andrew looked up at the deepening blue skies. An eagle swooped low over a grove of olive trees nestled against the rising hills. He said, "They stopped asking Jesus to leave soon enough, didn't they?"

"I should say," Peter answered his brother. "Just look at the people here. But I wonder how he can keep on, day after day, teaching and healing. He never turns the people away. And he knows when someone believes in him enough to receive his healing love. I'm thinking of that woman who followed him in the crowd the other day—the one healed just by touching the hem of his robe."

"I know," Andrew said. "The crowd was pressing against us on all sides as we walked through the streets. I heard Jesus say, 'Who touched me?' I couldn't understand why he had asked that question. Everyone was touching him, we were all so pushed against one another in the crowd.

"How Jesus knew by the touch alone that someone wanted to be healed, I can't figure out. But the trembling, sick woman came up and said she was the one who had touched him. And at once she was healed of the sickness she'd had for so many years. Did you hear our master Jesus tell her to go in peace, that her faith in him had made her whole?"

"Yes," Peter answered. "But do you know which healing amazed me the most?" Andrew shook his head. "It was the healing of the twelve-year-old girl—Jairus' daughter. There was so little hope that she would live. I was there when Jairus' messenger came. He asked Jesus to come to the house to help the girl. I also was there when the word came to us that she had already died. Weren't you surprised when Jesus went to the house after all? I really didn't think that he would. After all, we were too late. But Jesus wanted to go, anyway."

"One thing I remember clearly," said Andrew, "is the way all the people were crying and wailing when we reached the house. Families mourn the death of young people so deeply. It made me sad. But did you hear what Jesus said? He asked why they were acting that way."

Peter replied, "I heard that. The family was terribly confused. But not as confused, Andrew, as when Jesus said that the child was not dead, that she was only sleeping. No one believed him." A little smile touched Peter's mouth. "They even laughed at him. Remember?"

"I know. And it turned out that the girl really wasn't dead," Andrew said.

"I have to admit, Andrew, she looked dead to me. But Jesus just took the girl's hand and told her to sit up. She opened her eyes, got up from bed, and walked. I have never seen anything like that."

Peter gazed off across the calm blue waters of the Sea of Galilee. The sun slipped behind the trees crowning the hills. The evening air was filled with the delicious smells of the fruit trees. The tall fisherman looked worriedly at the sun, then at the crowds still gathered on the low, grassy hills. He said, "Those people should not wait any longer to go home for dinner. They should be leaving for their villages right now. Let's talk to Jesus about it."

Jesus turned to talk with the two disciples when they came up to him. Peter told Jesus what they were thinking: "It is getting late. Shouldn't we send the people into the villages for food? They need bread or meat or fish—something to eat that's heavier than the wild fruit here."

Jesus looked at his disciples. "There is no need for them to leave. You feed them."

"We will need many loaves of bread for all these people," Andrew said. "Do you want us to go and buy it?"

Jesus asked, "How many loaves of bread do we have?"

Peter turned to some other disciples nearby. He said, "Ask if anyone in the crowd has brought food along. You, Andrew, go over to that large group of people sitting in the shade of the olive trees. Surely someone has brought food for the children in that group. And you, James, ask those people sitting on the rocks near the shore."

As the disciples went from one group to another, Peter saw that they were finding no food. Andrew came back to his brother. He shook his head.

"There is nothing, Peter. No one has brought any food. The people will have to go into the villages to eat."

The big fisherman looked at his brother with a sure smile. "You do not believe enough, Andrew. Jesus said the people do not have to leave. And I have faith in him."

Behind the two brothers a young boy carrying a basket climbed over the rocks. He stooped down to look at some small fish trapped in a pool of water formed by the rocks near the shore. He caught two of the fish and put them into his basket. Then he walked up to Peter's side.

"Sir!" The boy looked up into Peter's weather-tanned face. The disciple did not hear the boy's quiet voice. He kept talking to Andrew. The boy tugged at the disciple's sleeve. "Sir," he said again.

Peter turned around. "Yes, what is it, boy?" he asked.

"I have five barley loaves my mother gave me this morning. And here are two little fish I caught. You may have them if you need them."

"Five loaves and two fish!" Andrew exclaimed. "That won't do much good. There are thousands of people."

"Just have faith, Andrew," Peter said. He looked down at the boy. "Thank you, son. This food will help. I will give the five loaves and the two fish to Jesus." Peter took the bread and fish in his big, rough hands, placed each into a separate basket, and walked up to Jesus.

Jesus took the food. Turning, he smiled at the little boy still standing by Andrew. Then Jesus told all of the people to sit down in groups spread out over the low, grassy hills by the shore. Holding the baskets of loaves and fish in his hands, he looked up to the skies and blessed the food.

Peter and the disciples took the bread and fish from Jesus and began to pass the food out to the crowds. There was enough for all the women, men, and children.

As the crowds finished eating, the disciples walked around, gathering up all the leftover pieces. There was so much that they filled twelve baskets with the uneaten food.

Just as the last light from the setting sun outlined the road, Jesus sent the people home. He waited until the last person had started toward the villages. Then he turned away from the shore and went up into the hills to be alone.

"Peter, are we to wait for him?" Andrew asked.

"No," Peter answered. The big fisherman stood just at the edge of the water near to where their boat was tied up. Waves lapped over his feet as he watched Jesus climbing the low hills in the deep blue dusk. "No, he is going alone to pray. He will meet us later."

Other disciples came up to help Peter and Andrew push the boat through the wet sand. Then they all leapt aboard as the hull slid free of the sand and drifted into deeper water. With the waves rocking them gently, they sailed out on the Sea of Galilee, turned silver gray in the twilight.

Peacefully the boat sailed late into the night. But a few hours after midnight a storm swooped down from the circling hills. The clouds grew dark, and mighty fists of wind struck the boat. Waves as high as six feet slashed against the men. "We must head into the wind!" Peter roared out as he fought to control the boat. "We'll capsize if we don't turn into the wind." Rain beat against the men's faces like slashing needles. Their clothes clung to them in cold, limp bunches.

"Peter, I've never seen a storm as bad as this," Andrew cried. "We will never make it to land!" The wind grabbed his words and tossed them away.

Peter did not answer because he had not heard. He was peering across the water. He squinted his eyes to see. His voice was low. "Andrew!"

"What is it?" Andrew asked. But Peter could not answer. He raised a trembling finger and pointed back toward the shore they had left. There, Andrew saw a figure walking across the tumbling waters. "A spirit!" Andrew cried out in fear. "A spirit is out here. It is coming to the boat."

The other disciples crowded in fright behind Andrew. "Where—what—where is it?" the questions came.

"See—over there!" Andrew pointed as Peter had done. The disciples, afraid, shrank back against one another.

Then the sound of a voice they knew and loved came to them. "Don't be afraid. It is I," Jesus said as he walked over the water toward the boat.

"Andrew, take over the boat," Peter said quietly. Then Peter stood up slowly in the bow. Looking toward the white figure just beyond the nearest wave, he said, "Master, if that is you, tell me to walk across the water to you."

"Come to me, Peter," Jesus said to the big fisherman. Peter slowly put one leg over the side of the boat. The wave tossed the craft up and down. "Come, Peter," Jesus said.

The fisherman stepped out onto the water and tried to walk toward Jesus. His eyes were on the face of his master. A wave splashed across his legs. He looked down and saw the churning gray waters. He felt the harsh wind beating against him. The big fisherman sank quickly down.

"Master, save me!" he cried out in a terrified voice. Storms were not new to the fisherman. Peter was able to handle himself in rain and high waves. But he was not standing on the deck of his boat now. He was in the water itself. "Save me, Jesus!" he called desperately.

Jesus reached out his hand and caught Peter. The master's strength lifted the disciple from the cold grasp of the sea.

"You have very little faith in me, Peter. Why did you doubt me?" Jesus asked. There was no answer from the big fisherman.

Jesus led Peter over the waves to the boat tossing heavily in the rough waters. As soon as they were in the boat, the wind and waves became calm. The boat rode as gently as ever on the Sea of Galilee.

The trembling disciples gathered around Jesus. A wet and shivering Peter stood gratefully beside the master. One by one, each disciple said, "Truly, Jesus, you are the Son of God!"

Jesus' teachings: Words to live by

The grass glistened in the early rising of the sun. The night's storm had washed away the dust from the green, leafy trees. As Jesus walked on the plain of Gennesaret, crowds of people followed him. Some had come to be taught, some to be healed—and still others came out of pure curiosity at Jesus' words and actions.

Among the curious people were some Pharisees from Jerusalem. The religious leaders had come to find out about this man from Nazareth. In the days ahead, the Pharisees would be puzzled by Jesus' words and by the way he acted. They followed only their own way of worshipping God, their own strict laws. Through the teachings of Jesus, many people were beginning to understand God's will differently from the way the Pharisees saw it.

A woman in the crowd handed some bread to Jesus' hungry disciples. Gratefully, they took the bread, broke it, and began to eat. The Pharisees were shocked. Angrily, they turned to Jesus and asked, "Why don't your disciples wash their hands before eating? That is one of God's laws."

Jesus turned to them. "You teach man-made laws, not those from God. It is not what goes into the mouth that makes a person unclean. It is what comes out of the mouth and what hides in the darkness of the heart: greed, hatred, and lies. These are the evil things that make one unclean.

"Pharisees, your hearts are far from pure. Don't believe that the way you act on the outside shows your closeness to God. Your soul is harmed only by what you think and say, not by anything you eat."

Peter walked up beside Jesus. "There is a house near here that will welcome us, Master. The family will give us food."

Peter pointed to a one-story house made of crude bricks. Then he led the way through a small courtyard to a wooden door. A water-storing tank just outside the house was filled to its brim with rain caught during the night's storm.

The family of the home welcomed Jesus and the disciples. They took the disciples' long cloaks and laid them to dry in the sun. Steam drifted up from the cloth, still damp from the night's rain that had poured down on the disciples as they had journeyed.

Peter took off his white turban and wiped his face. Loosening their leather sandals, all the disciples rested tired muscles. Jesus retied the long strip of linen that was wound several times around his waist. Over a white linen shirt he wore a short-sleeved tunic. The disciples wore the same simple clothing as their master.

"Our food is hot," the man of the house said. "It is plain food, but you are welcome to all you want."

Jesus and the disciples sat down on low wooden stools around a crude table. Jesus said to the man, "We know of no other kind of food. This meal is what we're used to. Most of my disciples are from the common people. Four are fishermen, menders of nets. And I am a carpenter. You have all the food we need, right here."

Jesus looked around the simple, one-room house. Dark brown clay mixed with straw made up the bricks for the walls. The floor of the room was hard-beaten dirt. "You have used the wood of the sycamore tree," Jesus said as he rubbed his hand over the rough table. He remembered the sycamore wood his father Joseph had used in the family's carpentry shop.

"Here is our food!" Peter happily rubbed his big hands

together. Jesus smiled at the look of joy on the big fisherman's face.

The wife set barley cakes on the table. The diners covered the flat bread with lentils, broad beans, and cucumbers. Onions and garlic added flavor to the dish. There were also big bowls of fresh figs on the table. The disciples hungrily reached for the food and broke bread with their hands.

As they ate, Jesus watched the man's wife set aside a little of the barley dough. She would mix this with the next day's dough to lighten, or leaven, it. The mixing made the bread turn out light and tasty.

Jesus said to his disciples, "Watch out for the leaven of the Pharisees and Sadducees. Just as this woman will mix dough for tomorrow with today's dough, so the Pharisees and Sadducees can mix in their false teachings with our faith."

The meal done, Jesus said, "Let us go up on the roof now. There are some things I must tell you."

The disciples got up from the table with many thanks to the woman and her husband for their kindness. Jesus led the way through the door to the outside steps going up to the roof. The flat top of the house was used for sleeping and recreation, and for prayer. The disciples settled themselves on the thickly plastered clay. Peter leaned against the low wall surrounding the roof.

Jesus began to teach his disciples as he often had before. "Do you remember what I told Nicodemus, the Pharisee, that night when he secretly came to me? You know he was a teacher of the Israelites, and he was faithful.

"Yet, he did not understand the ways of God. He had kept all the Pharisees' rules, but he had to start all over again in a new way of life with God in order to really know Him. The stiff, meaningless laws of the Pharisees crumble before God's love for every human being. I told Nicodemus that God loves all His people so much that He sent His only Son in order for life to be fuller than the people ever dreamed, in order for life to last forever."

Peter said, "And the Son of God is—"

"Yes, Peter?" Jesus looked at the sun-darkened fisherman. "Who is the Son of God?"

Peter answered, "You are the Christ, you are the Son of the Living God."

Jesus stood up. "You are blessed because God Himself has shown this to you. You are Peter, and on this rock I will build my church. All the powers in the world cannot stand against you. My church can grow upon this rock, upon a man like you."

But Jesus' next words brought a deep sadness to his disciples, for he began to tell them that he would die on the cross. Peter argued with his master. "No! This will not happen to you."

"Be silent, Peter, and listen. You are not thinking God's thoughts. You are thinking only as a man.

"God's kingdom will be known on earth through those who serve and sacrifice themselves. My death on the cross will show the way to give up life on this earth for the greater life God has promised us."

Peter turned away blindly. Angry tears burned his eyes.

"Come, Peter, and sit down. I must talk with you," Jesus said. The big fisherman turned slowly. He looked into the understanding eyes of his master. Peter sat down again.

Jesus said, "We cannot cherish anything more than the love we have from God—not warm, comfortable homes, rich clothing, or good food. Not even our lives. I am telling you, a camel could go through the eye of a needle more easily than a rich man with many possessions can enter the Kingdom of Heaven."

"Why is that?" a disciple asked.

"Because a rich man does not always share his wealth

with those in need. A rich man often begins to think too much of all the things he possesses. Often he feels that he alone is responsible for what he has. He forgets that all has come to him from God."

"We left our nets and boats, we left our families when you called us, Master. What more would you ask of us?" another disciple asked.

"Live each day being a servant to all, not by having others serve you. If you wish to be truly great, then every day give your life in service to others, just as I am going to give my life on the cross for God's people." Jesus stood up. He turned to hold out a helping hand to Peter. "Come with me now. It is time for us to be on our way. There are many people who need us to teach them, to heal them. And I do not have much time left to be with you."

Jesus and the disciples set out on the road to Jerusalem, to go to the temple there. At the end of the journey, facing the building, the disciples were awed by the costly gold and marble that had been used to decorate the front of it. Jesus walked through the crowds surging around him. He entered the temple, followed by his disciples in their simple linen tunics and shirts.

Walking in their long robes through the temple were proud scribes, the ones who explained God's Law for the Pharisees and the Sadducees. They meant their loud prayers to be heard by everyone. The high-ranking Sadducees walked through the arched doorways, not touching any of the common people for fear of becoming unclean in the eyes of God. They kept apart from the people, spending most of their time in the religious ceremonies of the temple.

While Jesus and the disciples stayed at the temple that day, teaching and healing, the chief priests and other leaders heard that even the children were praising Jesus. This upset the religious leaders. They decided to set traps to force Jesus into saying something they could use against him. The priests did not want to lose the people's loyalty to this new teacher.

Shoving a woman in front of the crowd, one Pharisee pushed her to her knees, into the dust. He pointed a finger at the woman and cried, "This woman has betrayed her lawful husband to be with another man. She must be stoned according to God's Law. Isn't that right, Jesus?"

The woman's body shook with her crying. Her long, dark hair hid the shame on her face.

Jesus did not look at the woman. He did not answer the question, either.

The Pharisee looked at Jesus impatiently. Again he said in a loud, accusing voice, "Shouldn't this woman be stoned? She has sinned." His long finger pointed at the woman on the ground.

Jesus looked at the woman, now cowering at his feet, grasping the hem of his robe. He looked at the people. Some pushed and shoved to see the woman and hear what Jesus would say. The ones nearby looked on, interested in what would happen. There were Pharisees there and common people, too. Even some Roman soldiers had taken an interest.

Jesus' voice came quietly to each woman and man: "If there is anyone here who has never sinned, then let that one be the first to throw a stone at this woman."

Silence fell over the crowd. The shoving for a place to see stopped. No one looked at anyone else. All heads were bowed. There was no one who could throw the first stone. There was no one without sin. No one but Jesus.

He looked at the woman, crouching at his feet. Jesus spoke to her: "Where are the people who accuse you? Hasn't even one of them condemned you?"

"No one, Sir," came her muffled voice.

"I do not condemn you, either. Go and sin no more." He held out his hand to help the woman up from the dust.

The Pharisees in the crowd were desperate to find a way to fight Jesus' influence. His power over the people was growing. Praises for his healing and teaching could be heard everywhere.

One tall Pharisee and his group thought that they had found the perfect plan for getting Jesus into trouble. The Pharisee said to Jesus, "I know you are honest and always teach the truth. They say you do so without fear, too. Now, tell us, is it right for us to pay taxes to Caesar, the emperor of Rome?"

This question was a dangerous one. The Jewish people felt the Roman tax was unfair. So, the Pharisees were trying to force Jesus to take a stand. If he said that the people should pay the tax, they would call Jesus a traitor.

But, if Jesus said they should not pay the tax, then the

Roman rulers would be angry. The soldiers would arrest him at once.

Jesus calmly said, "Bring me a coin."

Someone handed Jesus a penny as he stood before the crowd. The Pharisee in his long robe looked around at the people. A confident smile lined his mouth. He was sure Jesus could not answer without getting into trouble, either with the Jewish people or with the Romans.

"Whose face and writing are on this penny?" Jesus asked.

"Why Caesar's, of course," the Pharisee answered.

"Then, give back to Caesar what is his. He brought this Roman coin into this land. But also give to God what belongs only to Him."

There was nothing that the Pharisee could say or do. He had not trapped Jesus at all. The teacher from Nazareth would not get into an argument over taxes. His lesson was easy for the people to understand.

The tax should be paid to Caesar with Caesar's money, but to God each person should give what was God's: love and obedience. Jesus taught that people should look for the Kingdom of God and for God's goodness. Anything less than that was too small to worry about.

Again, the Pharisees sought to question Jesus. This time, one of their lawyers came to ask, "What is the greatest Commandment in God's Law?"

And the crowds, pressing around Jesus, heard him say, "You will love the Lord God with all your heart, and with all your soul, and with all your mind. This is the First Commandment and the greatest Commandment. And the second is to love your neighbor as you love yourself."

Jesus' words to live by reached out to each person in the crowd. Many heard and understood. But, sadly, some would never know the true meaning of the teachings of Jesus.

The Good Samaritan

"Jesus, how can I have eternal life?" This difficult question came to Jesus from a lawyer one day.

"If you want eternal life," Jesus answered, "you must love your God. That is one of our holy laws. But you must love your neighbor, too."

The lawyer still was not satisfied with Jesus' answer. He questioned further, "But who is my neighbor? The people who live next door to me? The people who are my friends? How about my enemies? Is everyone my neighbor?"

It was now that Jesus decided that what the lawyer and the people around him needed was to hear a parable, a simple story. The parable would clearly show everyone just what the word *neighbor* meant in God's law. This is how Jesus began:

The Jewish man lay under the skeleton branches of a dying olive tree. No green leaves shaded his bruised body from the stinging hot sun. His mouth was as dry as the torn shreds of his linen robe, lying beside him on the rocks.

From where he lay his moans of pain were too soft to be heard very far away. He could hear the tinkling bells of a flock of sheep somewhere above, but he was too weak to call more loudly for help.

This morning he had left Jerusalem just as the morning sun made long shadows of the olive groves. Mist was still lingering in the dips and hollows of the road. Then, as he came down a hill into this valley, four men stepped out of the whirls of the early morning mist.

They stood across the road, barring his way. The traveler

looked quickly behind him. No one else was coming along. He was alone before these four men.

"We'll take your money," a short, squat man said with a snarl. He jabbed out his dirty hand. The traveler stepped backward.

"The money, I said," the short man shouted. "And be quick, or you'll be sorry for being slow!"

The other thieves did not wait any longer. Two of them jumped on the traveler and knocked him to the ground. They grabbed his money and tore his clothes from his body. With sticks, they beat him until he fell on the rocks at the roadside. The four men then left without waiting to see if the traveler was alive or dead.

Now, much later, blood crusted over the cuts on the traveler's back, cuts left by the beating. He moved his face away from a sharp-edged stone cutting into his cheek. As the sun rose higher, there was not a sound. There was only the silence of the lonely road.

A small stone rolled—and another—and another. Someone, or something, was coming. The traveler was too weak to make even the softest cry for help. A sandal scraped along the side of the road near the injured traveler. But the steps did not stop! They quickly crossed the road away from the traveler lying in a bruised heap.

The man's eyes opened slowly. He could just see the shape of a figure hurrying away from him across the lane. It was a Jewish priest, a religious leader, coming down from Jerusalem—a religious leader who did not stop when he saw the injured figure, crumpled and bloody. The traveler gave a soft moan. The priest, afraid of being attacked himself, only quickened his steps down the road.

Very soon, even the sound of the sandals scuffing on the rocks faded. The traveler was left alone with the aching of his battered body. He licked his lips and tasted only the dry dust from the ground.

Slowly he rolled over on his side to get his face out of the dust. The pain of moving made him lose all thought and feeling for a while. Gnats buzzed around the cuts on his back and legs. As time passed, the sun rose until it stood right over him like a red-hot coal from an oven. He kept his eyes closed against the glare.

Suddenly a feeling came over him. He knew someone was looking down at him. Very slowly, he opened his eyes just a tiny slit. A black-bearded man stood right over him. His white turban dazzled in the sun. He held his spotless white robe back from the traveler's bloody wounds.

The injured man saw he was being watched by a Jew from the tribe of Levi. Help would surely come from a Levite, whose life was given to serving the priests. But the Levite did not stoop to help. He stared, looked quickly around, and, afraid, suddenly hurried off down the road. The dying away of his running footsteps left an emptier silence than ever.

Tears of weakness and pain blinded the injured man's eyes. Shuddering sobs filled his body with pain. He would die. There was no one who would help him, not even his own people. The thieves might come back to beat him again. Animals might crawl up to him when night came. His legs quivered as pain streaked down them from his back.

A cup of cool water held to his mouth suddenly shocked him. His eyes jerked open to see yet another man stooping beside him. "Here. Just a sip now," the broad-shouldered fellow said gently. "Just a swallow at a time."

The wounded traveler let the cool water trickle down his throat. He stared at the man holding the cup.

"They gave you a rough time," the man said. "Just lie still now. I'll take care of these cuts first."

Water gently washed away the dust and grit from the traveler's wounds. He mumbled, "Who . . . ?"

"Quiet now. Just rest easy. I'm from Samaria. I was on my way to the Jordan River when I heard your moans. I almost missed seeing you."

Thoughts tumbled in the injured man's head. A Samaritan had stopped to help a Jew? Samaritans were not even treated as friends of the Jews. Yet, a Samaritan had stopped. And where was that priest now—and that Levite, the servant of the priests? They were both safely on their way.

"Can you turn over slowly? I want to treat your wounds with this oil and wine. Gently, now," the Samaritan said. Then he cleaned and treated each cut. Soon the Samaritan slowly helped the Jewish traveler to sit up.

"We cannot stay here. It is not safe. I am going to help you up on my donkey. Then I will take you to an inn I know farther down the road. Hold onto me, now, and try to stand," the Samaritan said.

Pains shot through every muscle as the traveler struggled to stand. The Samaritan's strong, muscular arms steadied him and lifted him up on the donkey's back. Leading the animal, the Samaritan started down the rock-filled road.

After a painful ride of several miles, they reached a cool grove of trees. Here, set back from the road, was an inn. The Samaritan lifted the Jew and carried him inside.

"A room, a clean bed, and some warm food. Hurry!" the Samaritan called to the innkeeper.

Through the rest of the day and that night the Samaritan took care of the injured man. He treated the man's cuts with oil and wine a second time. He spooned warm vegetable soup into the Jew's mouth.

By morning the traveler felt some strength coming back to his body. As he opened his eyes from a heavy sleep, he saw the Samaritan getting ready to leave.

The Samaritan looked at him and said, "I'm glad to see you so much better. But you are not ready to travel yet." He turned and handed some money to the innkeeper standing at the door. "Look after him now. Spend whatever you need for him. When I come back this way, I will repay you.

"Take care of yourself, Neighbor," he said to the Jew. And the Good Samaritan was gone on his way.

This was the end of Jesus' story. He turned to the lawyer, the one who had questioned him earlier, and said, "Tell me, do you understand now what the word *neighbor* means? Can you tell me now, of the three men who saw the traveler wounded by the thieves, which one was a neighbor to the injured man?"

The lawyer answered, "It was the man who showed mercy and kindness to the traveler."

Jesus looked steadily at the lawyer and said, "Then you go and do the same."

The Prodigal Son

Many people gathered in the open air to hear Jesus speak. Most of the crowd waited patiently and quietly, but a mumbling and buzzing soon began among a dozen or so people. Finally, the little group came close to where Jesus stood. They were Pharisees and scribes, Jewish religious leaders and scholars.

One of them said, "We believe in your ideas about being good and following God's Law, Jesus. But have you looked at some of the people who are here today? This crowd is filled with sinful people. Why are you wasting your time talking to them? Why don't you tell them to leave? They have no right to be here with good people."

Jesus listened patiently. Then, gently, he said, "Suppose you had a hundred sheep, and one day one of them was lost? What would you do?"

"Why, I'd go look for it, of course," the man said.

"And when you found that lost sheep, you'd take it back to the flock. Isn't that right?"

"I would," the man said. "But what has that to do with the sinners here?"

Jesus held out his hands. "Don't you see? A shepherd is overjoyed to find a lost lamb and return it to the fold. Doesn't it follow that the angels of God rejoice when one lost soul is found?"

The speaker shrugged. Jesus stepped a little closer. "Or consider a situation like this: a woman has ten silver coins, but one day when she counts them, one is missing. Quickly, she lights a lamp and begins a search through every corner of the house. And, suddenly, there it is, rolled into a dark corner. Joyfully, the woman holds the coin to the light and calls to her friends, 'Come, help me give thanks! I thought my coin was lost, but here it is.' "

Jesus glanced from one face in the group to the next. "If someone is overjoyed at the return of so small a thing as a coin, imagine the happiness in heaven when a sinner creeps out from the dark corners and comes to God."

Then Jesus looked out at the crowd. There were parents there with small children. There were rich men standing proudly in brightly colored robes. There were women speaking softly while breezes rippled their long garments. And there were beggars, dressed in rags, crouched apart from the others as though fearful of being driven away.

The people sensed that Jesus was about to speak to them again. A hush fell and, in a calm voice, Jesus began. His voice was gentle, but it carried to the far reaches of the audience: "Let's talk today about people who are lost and people who are found again. And let's talk about forgiveness," he said. "I'd like to tell you a story."

The crowd leaned forward eagerly. "There was a man, a fairly rich man, who had two sons. One day the younger son said, 'Father, I wish you'd divide up your property now so that I could have my share while I'm still young enough to enjoy it.'

"The father, thinking, perhaps, that the boy wanted to learn how to manage on his own, agreed. But the son lost no time in selling everything his father had given him. Then he left home with the money.

"The wasteful, or prodigal, son went to a faraway land and began spending his money wildly. Before long, he had spent it down to the last coin. Then a famine came to the country. People had next to nothing to eat.

"The young man—who had been so carefree—was now in great trouble. He traveled from place to place, trying to earn money, but people would just look at him and say, 'How can we help you? We have nothing ourselves.'

"Finally, the young man did find a job, but it was a lowly one. He worked for a farmer, feeding and caring for pigs. In the opinion of his countrypeople, this job was one of the worst anyone could have. As the wasteful son shoveled out bean pods for the animals to eat, he could not help thinking that the pigs ate better than he did.

"One evening, as he stood in the mud and grime near the pens, he brushed his hands along his sides and felt his ribs through his worn and dirty clothes. 'What a fool I am,' he thought. 'The people who work on my father's farm have all kinds of food, and here I am, wasting away. I don't know how much longer I can go on like this.'

"Then he thought some more about how he had tossed aside his pleasant life just for fun and adventure. Now all he had was hunger and sorrow. 'I'll go back to my father,' he murmured. 'I'll say to him, "Father, I have sinned against God and against you. I am no longer fit to be called your son. Treat me as one of your hired workers." '

"The wasteful son left for home at once, while he still had strength enough to travel. The young man was still some distance from home when news of his return reached the father. Overjoyed, the old man went out to meet his younger child. He threw his arms around the young man.

"The son almost wept with relief and happiness, but he blinked back the tears and in a firm voice said what he had planned to say: 'Father, I have sinned against God and against you. I am no longer fit to be called your son.'

"But the father put his finger against his son's lips. 'You're still my son, no matter what,' the father said. 'And this is a day of great happiness for me because you've come home at last.' Then the father turned to the servants who had followed him and said, 'Hurry, bring the best robe in the house and put it on my son. Put a ring on his finger

and shoes on his feet. Then find the fattest calf in the lot and prepare a feast. My son was dead, but now he's alive. He was lost, but now he's been found.'

"The servants hurried off and by the time the father and son reached the house, the celebration had already begun.

"Meanwhile, the older son finished his work in the field and started towards home. He heard sounds of music and, even from a distance, he could see dancing figures. Confused, he turned to one of the servants. 'Run ahead,' he told the servant. 'Find out what's going on.'

"As the older son neared the house, the servant came dashing out. 'Good news! Your brother has returned.'

" 'My brother!' A rush of anger surged through the older son. 'That good-for-nothing!'

" 'And there's all kinds of feasting taking place,' the servant said. 'And music. Listen to the music!'

"Instead, the older brother slumped angrily under a tree. Finally, his father came out and stood before him. 'My son,' he said, 'what are you doing out here? Why aren't you inside, so you can celebrate with the rest of us?'

"The young man stood up and faced his father. 'Celebrate? Why should I celebrate! This isn't fair,' he said. 'All this time I've worked hard and done everything you've asked. But this other son—my younger brother—what does he do? He takes his money and throws it around and disgraces the family. And then, when he's down and out, he comes home. And you treat him like your favorite.'

"The father put his hands on his older son's shoulders and said, 'You are a good and loyal son, and I love you with all my heart. But let me be happy this day and celebrate. Don't you see that your brother was dead and he was brought back to life? He was lost and has been found!'

"The older son saw the pleading look in the old man's kind face. He could no longer be angry. He took his father's arm and, together, they walked into the house."

The Unkind Servant

One day Peter approached Jesus. "Something has been troubling me," he said, "and I need your opinion."

"Tell me about it, and I will try to relieve your mind," Jesus said, in a gentle, encouraging way.

Peter hesitated a moment, then cleared his throat and said, "You speak a lot about forgiveness. Now, of course, I agree that forgiving faults and sins is the right thing to do. But just how far does one need to go? For example, if my brother keeps on sinning against me, would you say that I should forgive him as many as seven times?"

"No, not seven times," Jesus answered. "You should forgive your brother seventy times seven."

"Seventy times seven!" Peter shook his head in surprise.

"Forgiveness shouldn't have any limits," Jesus said. "It should flow on and on, from day to day, like a great river. And its goodness should touch everyone, not just a few. Would you like to hear an example of what I mean?"

The disciples, always eager to hear a story, arranged themselves around a flat rock where Jesus had sat down. It was a quiet place where they were, and out in the open air. But Jesus' story took them to a different place, to the vast hall of a king's throne room. Jesus began the story this way:

The hall was on the chilly side—damp and drafty because the warmth of the sun never made its way through the thick stone walls. The only light came from torches attached to the walls. And, in the upper air, wisps of smoke mingled with the scent of incense.

Sometimes the king held feasts here in honor of visitors from other lands. Then there was a great deal of merriment and bustling about in the throne room. Servants brought out platters of food to eat and goblets of wine to drink. On certain days, however, there was a far different feeling in the room. These were the times when those accused of committing a crime had to explain themselves to the king.

One day the king heard rumors that one of his highly placed servants had been stealing from the king's own stores of money. It seemed that for some time the servant had cleverly taken money from the royal budget and put it into his own pocket. This man was so sneaky, in fact, that he had gotten away with thousands in cash. When he came to trial, the evidence proved that he was guilty.

The king clutched the carved arms of the throne and leaned forward. "I trusted you," he said, his voice husky with anger. "You have been a favored servant in the royal household, and in return I see you have betrayed my trust."

The servant gave a shudder. He had never seen the king in so cold a rage. He felt his insides twisting into knots. He was guilty and, having no defense, he was almost sure he would be put to a horrible death. He raised his eyes and tried to speak, but no words would come out.

The king, seeing the terror on the man's face, calmed a little. But, still, he could not let this criminal go free. The man had to be punished.

"I don't want you around here any more," the king finally said. "I order you to be sold as a slave. And I will have your wife and children sold, too, and everything you own. Then maybe I'll get at least some of the money back that you owe me."

"Oh, please, please be merciful," the servant begged. "I've done a great wrong, but won't you show forgiveness? If you'll just give me a chance, I swear I'll work my fingers to the bone to pay you back every bit of money I've taken." He lifted his eyes to the king. "I beg you," he repeated, "spare me and my loved ones in the name of mercy and goodness!"

Stroking his beard, the king looked at the servant. In the little circle around the throne all were silent, waiting. Finally, with a sigh, the kind-hearted king said, "All right. I believe you're sincere, and I think you have learned your lesson. Let no one say I'm a harsh and unforgiving ruler. I can show forgiveness in a worthy case." He motioned to a guard, who pulled the man to his feet.

The servant brushed off his robes and left the room. Once outside, he quickly lost his fear and began to feel that he was a clever man, indeed. Not only had he stolen, but he had gotten away with it, too.

He strolled into the courtyard, glancing here and there at the people milling about. Suddenly, he spied another of the king's servants standing with two other men. This servant had borrowed money from the first servant some time ago and had never paid it back.

"Hey, there!" shouted the first servant. "Where have you been lately? You've been avoiding me, haven't you?"

The second servant came forward. "I haven't been avoiding you," he said. "The fact is, I haven't got your money. But I'll have it soon, and then I'll pay you back, believe me."

"You liar!" the first servant shouted. "You have no intention of paying me back. You're just a common, ordinary thief." He lunged toward the man and began choking him. "Thief! Thief!" the first servant kept shouting. The two tumbled to the ground and wrestled in the dust.

Some of the king's guards rushed up and pulled the men apart. "He stole my money!" the first servant shouted as the guards pried his fingers from the second man's throat. "Throw him into jail until he pays!" The guards dragged

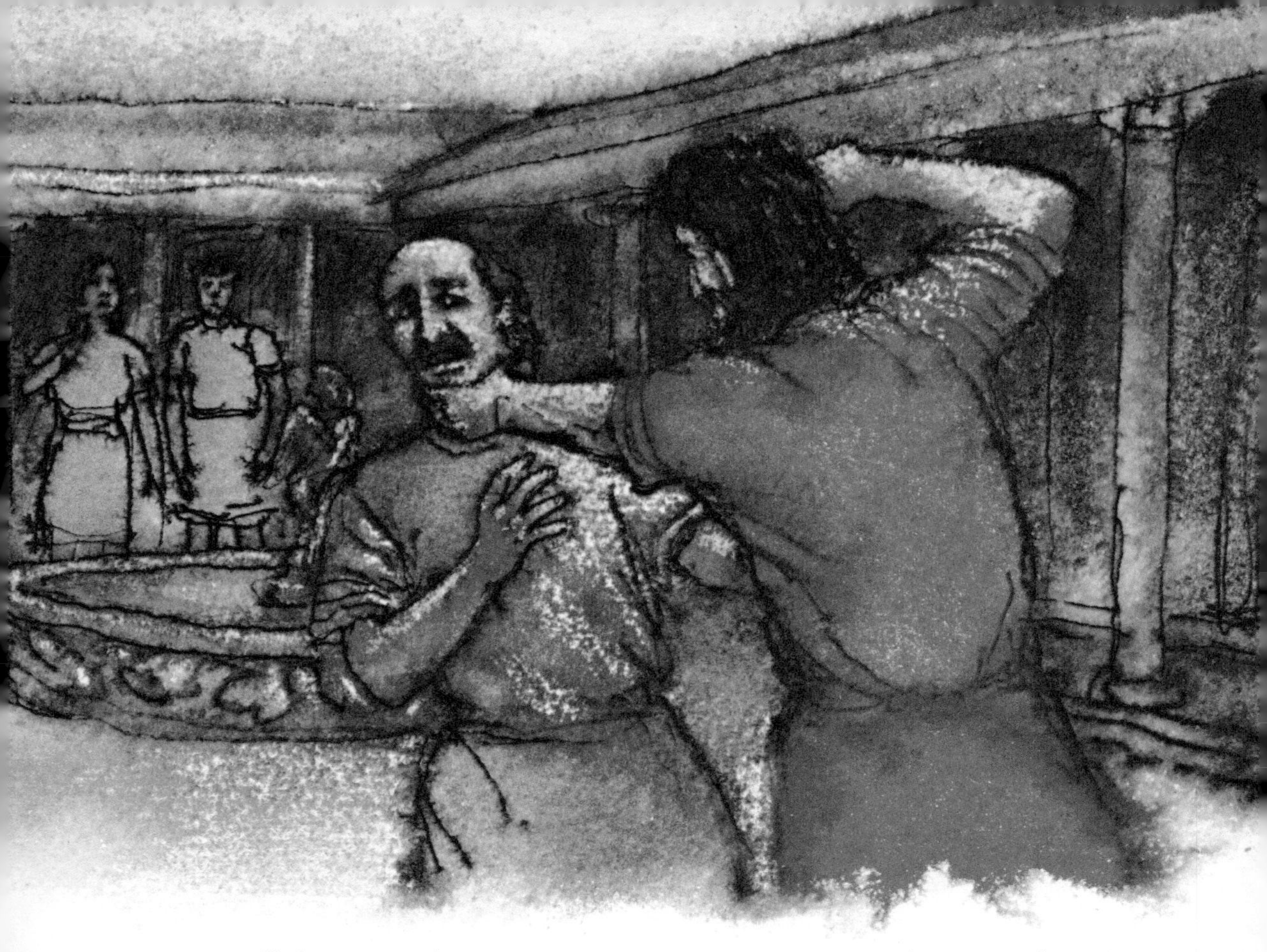

off the second servant, paying no attention to his cries for mercy.

Meanwhile, the men who had been talking to the second servant wrung their hands in sympathy and complained about the rough treatment given to their friend. Their complaints turned into pure anger a few moments later when a witness from the royal chamber came up and told what had recently taken place before the king. "Can you believe it?" the witness said, pointing to the first servant. "The king just forgave that man a huge debt. Then the scoundrel turns right around and has a fellow servant thrown into jail."

The two friends, waiting to hear no more, rushed into the hall. They begged permission to tell the king how cruel the first servant was.

"That wicked man stole from your own budget, Your

Majesty," they said, "and you forgave him. But he himself shows no mercy to the servant who owes him money."

The king was furious. "Bring him back here!" he ordered. "Now he's really going to be punished."

This time the guards flung the first servant to the floor in front of the king. They looked as though they wanted to beat him.

"Don't ever ask me again for forgiveness," the king said in a cold voice, standing straight and tall at his throne. His eyes blazed as he looked down on the cringing form. "I went easy on you before, but since you didn't have the decency to pass that kindness along, you're going to suffer."

The king turned to the guards. "Take this man to jail and punish him," he commanded. "Keep him locked up until he pays back the whole amount he owes me."

This was where Jesus ended his story. For a few moments, the disciples looked thoughtful. Then, one of them asked, "Would it be correct, Jesus, to compare the king to God in heaven, Who forgives even the greatest of sins?"

"Yes, that is correct," Jesus answered.

"And we are the servants," Peter added, "who should forgive one another. But that isn't always easy, you know." Peter frowned. "And then, what you said before about forgiving someone more than seven times, about forgiving someone seventy times seven. That's a lot of forgiving."

There was a silence, and then Peter shrugged. "Well, seventy times seven is four hundred and ninety times. If you forgive someone four hundred and ninety times, I suppose it could become a habit."

Jesus looked at Peter and smiled. But he did not reply.

Sermon on the Mount

It is no wonder that Jesus' teachings had such an effect on the people. He spoke simply and directly, especially compared to the Pharisees, the religious leaders.

Because Jesus was so patient in explaining ideas, and because he gave hope and understanding to so many people, the crowds that followed him grew larger every day. Jesus simply could not reach all those who came to him from miles around. At first, he tried preaching from a boat, so that all the people could see and hear him. But even this was not enough. Jesus needed some helpers.

Jesus chose them from among the people who had been following him closely. Their names were Simon Peter, Andrew, James and John, Philip of Bethsaida, and Bartholomew. Also, there was Thomas and Matthew, another James, another Simon, Jude, and Judas Iscariot. We call these special helpers the twelve apostles of Jesus.

At first, Jesus' instructions to the apostles were simple. He said that they should be with him whenever they could. But, at times, he would also send them out to preach in the places he could not cover if he worked alone. Jesus told them to follow his own ways of teaching. He also gave them the power to heal sickness and disease.

Then, Jesus took the apostles up onto a mountain so that he could tell them more things they had to know in order to carry out his work. Some people followed Jesus and the apostles up the mountainside. These people did not know it, but they were about to receive an important message. The message was a sermon: the Sermon on the Mount.

In the calm silence, Jesus told his twelve new helpers what kind of people he expected them to be. "You are the salt of the earth," he said. "But you must be careful to protect your value. Because if salt loses its taste, it's of no use to anyone. It might as well be thrown upon the ground and trampled underfoot.

"You are like light for the whole world. A light is meant to shine forth and chase away the shadows. In the same way, your light must shine before people so that they can see the good things that you do and thank their Father in heaven."

One of the apostles turned to another and whispered. They both looked puzzled. "It looks as though something is troubling you," Jesus said.

"Just this," the first apostle replied. "Are we to forget the old laws? Is there a new set to follow?"

"Not at all," Jesus answered. "I haven't come to do away with the Law of Moses or the teachings of the prophets. I have come to put them into effect. It's still true that anyone who disobeys the Commandments or talks someone else into breaking them will be of low standing in the Kingdom of Heaven. But, if you follow the Commandments and set a good example for others, you'll have a high place in that same Kingdom of Heaven."

A man who had been listening from a short distance moved forward now. "Jesus," he said, "what happens when I obey the Commandments, but my friends don't?" The man's face became red with anger now, and he clenched his fists. "I'd just love to lay my hands on one of my neighbors, to get even for something he did to me."

Jesus looked patiently at the man. "Anger is as bad as the evil deed itself," he said in a mild tone. "People used to believe in the saying, 'An eye for an eye and a tooth for a tooth.' But now I tell you that is wrong. If someone slaps your cheek, turn the other cheek. If someone demands your shirt, give him your coat, as well. Give good for evil, and treat others as you would want them to treat you."

The angry man looked bewildered. "I don't think you understand what I'm trying to say. This man is my enemy. You talk as though I should actually love him."

"You should," Jesus said. "Remember, it's easy to love your friends. Why shouldn't you love them? They are good to you. But it's hard to love people who have done you some wrong. Yet, this is what you must do: love and forgive your enemies if you expect God to forgive you your own sins.

"Pray for those who torment you, so you may become the son of your Father in heaven. He makes His sun shine on the bad and the good people, and He makes the rain to fall on those who do evil as well as good. So you, too, should be merciful to both the fair and the unfair people. In other words, try to be perfect, as your Father in heaven is perfect."

An apostle touched the sleeve of Jesus' robe. "Speaking of perfect, look at that saintly person over there." He pointed to a bearded man in scarlet robes who was passing out money to beggars. "Now, that man knows the meaning of giving."

Jesus walked towards the clearing where the rich man stood, proud and aloof as he tossed coins to the ground. "Do you really believe that man to be kind and generous?" Jesus asked.

"Why, to be sure." The apostle looked at Jesus' unsmiling face. "But, then again . . ." he mumbled, confused.

"The person who gives in public is doing it for show, not because he has a good heart," Jesus said. "If you really want to help someone in need, you should do so in private. You should not brag about it. You should not tell even your closest friend. Go out of your way to help and support anyone in trouble, and then be sure to keep the good deed to yourself. Your Father, Who sees what you do in private, will bless you for it."

"Is prayer a private matter, too?" John asked. "It seems it should be. But then, everyone thinks people are quite holy when they stop in the streets or in places of worship and raise their arms and their voices to the glory of God."

"Don't be impressed," Jesus said. "It's only a performance. Hypocrites can carry on in public and make a big show. But, if you had the power to look into their hearts, you'd see their holiness is all a fake."

By now, men and women and youngsters followed Jesus and his apostles as they moved along the grassy slopes of the mount. The crowd pressed ever closer to catch every word Jesus spoke. "How, then, shall we pray?" came the soft voice of a woman.

Jesus paused and turned. His eyes swept over the cluster of eager faces before him. "First, go into a room and close the door," he said. "Pray to your Father, Who is unseen, but Who hears your words—even when they are still in your heart. It isn't necessary to run on and on with words that mean nothing. This is how you should pray:

Our Father, Which art in heaven,
Hallowed be Thy name.
Thy kingdom come
Thy will be done
In earth, as it is in heaven.
Give us this day our daily bread,
And forgive us our debts,
As we forgive our debtors.
And lead us not into temptation,
But deliver us from evil.

For thine is the kingdom, and the power,
and the glory, for ever. Amen.

As the beauty and simplicity of the words filled their souls, there was a silence in the little crowd that had gathered. Some faces were old and lined with age. Some were strong with health. There were mothers holding infants, and there were children who had stopped the games of youth to stand motionless, listening to the words of the man before them in white robes. Suddenly, a little boy of about nine, who had been hanging about on the edge of the crowd, came forward. He stood before Jesus and looked at him with large, dark, and somewhat frightened eyes.

"Yes, lad, what is it?" the gentle question came, for Jesus loved children. "Do you wish to ask me something?"

"About forgiveness." The boy swallowed hard. "My family is poor," he said. "And, for that reason, some of the boys tease me and even throw stones." He blinked back the tears in his eyes. "Must I forgive them?"

"If you forgive them, your heavenly Father will forgive you," Jesus said. "It isn't easy, but that is what you must try to do. And then, in turn, He will forgive you at those times when you do something wrong."

A man who had drifted forward put his hands on the shoulders of the young boy standing before Jesus. "I'm this boy's father," he said, "and I'm sorry for everything he's going through. But, you see, times are hard for us. I worry from one day to the next where I'll find the money to feed and clothe my family."

Jesus answered, "Do the best you can, but don't waste your life in worry. Isn't life more than food? And isn't the body worth more than clothes? Look upwards!" Jesus raised his arm towards birds swooping in the sky. "See how carefree they are? Birds don't plant seeds or gather harvests, and yet their needs are cared for by our Father in heaven."

As the man's fingers picked the loose, ragged edges of

his garment, Jesus added, "As for your clothes, what do they matter? Look at the flowers blooming over there. If you would really stop to examine them, you'd realize they're more beautiful than even the richest clothes King Solomon wore on great occasions. So don't be concerned about material things, things that can be bought and sold. Instead, give your attention to the things of the spirit. That's where real beauty lies."

Then Jesus told the crowd, "Ask, and you will receive. Seek, and you will find. Knock, and the door will be opened to you. Would any of you who are mothers or fathers give your children a stone if they asked for food? Of course not. Somehow, you will give your children what they need. And your Father in heaven will do even more."

The sun was beginning to lower, and a faint chill crept into the air. The people clutched their clothing close to them. But still they lingered, waiting to catch every word that Jesus said.

Jesus looked at each apostle in turn and then let his gaze sweep over the people before him. "You must prepare yourselves for the day when you are called to God. Anyone who hears my words and takes them to heart is like someone who builds a house upon a rock. When the rains come and the winds blow, the house stands straight and sound because it is built on a solid base. But if you hear my words and do not obey them, you're like the foolish person who builds a house on sand. The rains and winds blow it down, and all is lost. As you leave today, remember my words, and build your life accordingly. The good and the strong and the honest will be saved."

As Jesus finished speaking, the crowd slowly and silently made its way down from the mount. The Sermon on the Mount was over, and the listeners had many new things to think about.

Although Jesus had spoken freely to the crowds, there

was one subject that he always saved for his apostles alone. This subject was what would happen to him in the future. Jesus knew that he would be brought to trial and that he would suffer and die.

The apostles were troubled when Jesus talked about his approaching death. Peter, in particular, almost refused to accept the fact that his master would die in pain. But Jesus insisted: "Don't doubt my words, Peter. Believe me, it will all happen. And you will have to share my suffering in one way or the other if you are going to be loyal to me."

Jesus, knowing how hard Peter was struggling, took him to the top of the mountain to pray. James and John also went along.

When the three apostles reached the top, they saw a strange and wonderful thing. The figure of Jesus became radiant and glowing. Even his robes became so white they almost blinded the surprised apostles.

And then, from the misty clouds of the mountain appeared the forms of Moses and the prophet Elijah. They had come from death to talk with Jesus.

Then the mists brightened, and out of the mists came the voice of God Himself, saying, "This is My beloved Son, in whom I am well pleased. Listen to him."

In the dark days ahead, Peter would be comforted by what he had seen during those radiant moments on the mountaintop with Jesus, Moses, and Elijah. And he would be strengthened by the wisdom of the Sermon on the Mount.

From now on, Peter would never doubt the gentle master. And he would love Jesus with all his heart.

Jesus raises Lazarus from death

In the time of Jesus, there were not very many inns, or hotels, where tired wanderers could rest. So, it was a custom in those days for people to take travelers into their home. Being kind to strangers was considered an act as holy as giving money to the poor. Even if the people who knocked at the door for food and lodging were enemies, they were taken inside and cared for. Because of this custom, Jesus and his apostles were free to wander about, preaching the word of God. They knew that when night came they would be given food and shelter.

Nowhere did Jesus find a warmer welcome than in the home of Mary, Martha, and their brother Lazarus. The three lived in the small town of Bethany, a suburb not far from the holy city of Jerusalem.

Mary, Martha, and Lazarus lived in an especially comfortable house with large, airy rooms and an enclosed courtyard. When Jesus arrived there the first time, he was welcomed and taken in as a courtesy because he was a traveler. But soon the family members realized that he was no ordinary traveler. As the sisters and brother spoke to Jesus, they were amazed by his goodness and his wisdom. They urged him to return whenever he could, and they looked forward to his visits eagerly.

One day when Jesus was several days' journey from Bethany, a messenger came with this news: "Lord, your friend Lazarus, whom you love, is very ill." It had taken the messenger several days to reach Jesus. Lazarus was at this point already near death. But Jesus did not go to

Lazarus. Instead, he sent the messenger on his way and continued preaching.

Then, a day or so later, Jesus said to his apostles, "Our friend Lazarus has fallen asleep. I will go to wake him up."

"Sleep is good," the apostles pointed out. "Why not just let Lazarus rest?"

"I meant the long sleep," Jesus said. "Lazarus is dead. But for your sake—for the sake of your belief—I'm glad I wasn't there. Come now, I will show you what I mean. We must go to Bethany."

For days, worried friends in Bethany had been watching the road for the arrival of Jesus. He was their one hope of saving Lazarus. But, suddenly, it was too late. Lazarus died before Jesus arrived.

The sisters were heartbroken. With cries of sorrow, they watched while their beloved brother's body was washed, touched with precious oils, and wrapped in linens. Then, the same day Lazarus died, his friends sealed his body away in the family tomb. They rolled a huge stone before the cavelike entrance.

Lazarus' sisters believed, as was the custom in those days, that a dead person's spirit hovered on earth for three days. On the fourth, the spirit departed. Then, the death was final.

On the fourth day after Lazarus' death, a few villagers from Bethany saw Jesus coming towards the town. They hurried to tell Martha. She slipped away from the mourners gathered in the house and hurried out to meet Jesus at the edge of town. "Lord," she cried, "if you had only been here, my brother would not have died!" She fell at the feet of Jesus, weeping bitterly.

Jesus knelt and gently touched Martha. She blotted the tears from her cheeks with the edge of her veil. "Your brother will rise again," Jesus said in a soft, comforting tone.

Martha raised her head. With the trusting look of a child, she said, "I know he will rise again on the Day of Judgment, when God ends the world."

"I am the resurrection and the life," Jesus said softly. "Whoever believes in me will live, even in death. Do you accept that as the truth?"

"Oh, yes, Master, I do!" Martha exclaimed.

There was a moment of peaceful silence. Then Jesus murmured, "Bring your sister Mary here."

Martha went back to the house and found her sister as she had left her, head bowed, weeping with the other mourners. Martha leaned over and whispered, "The Master is here and asks for you." For a moment, a look of hope flickered over Mary's face. But then the thought came: My brother is four days dead. Even his spirit no longer hovers at the tomb. Still, Mary loved Jesus dearly and trusted him. She hurried after Martha.

When Mary saw Jesus standing near a grove of olive trees, she rushed forward, and, as Martha had done, knelt at his feet. Her words, like her sister's, showed her strong belief and devotion. "Oh, Master," she gasped between her sobs, "if you had only been here, our brother would not have died."

Her grief was so heartbreaking that Jesus himself wept. "Where have you buried him?" Jesus asked the bowed figure of Mary.

Rising, she said, "Come, we will show you."

The two sisters moved in the direction of the cave, and Jesus walked between them along the winding path. Mourners trailed behind the three. Some whispered, "See how he loved Lazarus. He's going to the tomb to mourn."

But others murmured, "What does he expect to do now, at this late date? Of course, if he had arrived sooner, he might have prevented this death. I understand he has even made the blind see again."

They finally reached Lazarus' tomb. The huge boulder still stood before the entrance, sealing it. "Remove the stone," Jesus commanded.

Everyone looked at him in astonishment. Martha said, "Oh, but Master! He has been dead four days!"

Jesus looked at her steadily. "Did I not say to you that if you would believe, you would see the glory of God?" Martha nodded, unable to speak.

Mary, who had such absolute belief in Jesus that she would never question him, no matter what, made a sign to the mourners. Strong men went to the entrance of the cave and, with great effort, they began to move the stone away, prying it back inch by inch.

A hush fell over the little group. Eyes peered first towards the dark, inner depths of the tomb, showing more and more as the men moved the stone away. Then the eyes swept to the face of Jesus. Raising his face to heaven so that everyone would know where his strength and power lay, Jesus said, "I pray aloud, Father, so that all who hear may believe that You have sent me. The hour is coming when the dead will hear the voice of God."

Filled with the Holy Spirit, Jesus was ready to demonstrate the truth of those words. Lowering his eyes, he looked into the tomb. "Lazarus," he cried, "come forth." There were gasps. The onlookers shrank back.

Silence. Then suddenly Lazarus appeared at the entrance of the opening tomb. He was wrapped in strips of white burial linen. His head was still covered with a grave cloth. He reached up and removed it. His face looked as it had when he was in perfect health. The sisters looked from Lazarus to Jesus and back to Lazarus. "Unwrap him," Jesus said to the onlookers, who were motionless with shock. "And let him go home."

They removed the burial garments. Lazarus, though a bit dazed, looked strong and healthy. Mary and Martha, whose eyes were now overflowing with tears of joy, took their brother back home.

Many of the mourners who had seen this great miracle take place praised Jesus. They confessed their faith in him as the true Son of God. But a few drifted off and whispered among themselves. With narrowed eyes, they watched Jesus. "This man is dangerous," they decided. "Something must be done about him." And they went straight to the Pharisees to report what they had seen.

Martha, Mary, and Lazarus celebrated the miracle of Lazarus' return to life. They did not know that at that same moment enemies were plotting against Jesus. They did not know that Jesus, bringing Lazarus back from death, would die himself in only a short while.

Judas betrays Jesus

The Jewish high priests and the Pharisees were becoming more and more uneasy about Jesus' power over their people. Finally, the two groups called a meeting.

"This man is becoming too popular," a speaker for the Pharisees began. "If we let him keep on preaching, all the people will soon follow him. Already they are calling him a king, the King of the Jews. The Romans are going to get angry. If this keeps up, they'll close down our temple and maybe even punish us. All of us."

"We agree," came the high priests' reply. "This Jesus is dangerous. But what can we do to stop him?"

Caiaphas, who was head of the high priests, snorted. "What can we do?" He looked from one face to another. "There's only one thing to do. Kill him."

The Pharisees and other high priests rubbed their hands together, worried. Surely there was another way.

Caiaphas leaned forward. "Don't you see? It's the only thing we can do. I have nothing against this Jesus personally, but I'm certainly not going to sit back and let him ruin all of us. Only by getting rid of this preacher can we save ourselves and all our people from the Romans."

"How shall we do it?" asked one of the crowd. "When?"

"The feast of the Passover will soon be here," Caiaphas said, "and that's not a good time. Jesus is a preacher, a popular religious leader. And he has committed no crime. The people would be in a big uproar if we killed him during Passover. We'll have to wait until after the holiday." Caiaphas stood up and stretched. "And for how we kill him, well, that shouldn't be difficult. Death is easy to arrange. Think about it. And have a nice holiday." With that, Caiaphas left the room.

Jesus knew that people were plotting against him and that he did not have much time left on earth. Still, his work went on. He wandered about in his usual way, preaching wherever a crowd gathered. Then, as the feast of the Passover drew closer and closer, Jesus told his apostles that it was time to start southward towards Bethany, to the home of Mary, Martha, and Lazarus.

"I have much to tell to you along the way," he said, "to prepare you to continue my work when I am no longer here." The apostles were uneasy when Jesus spoke of leaving them, but, still, they listened eagerly to all their master had to say.

One noon during their journey, after they had paused to take refreshment under the calm, leafy branches of an especially lovely tree, Jesus said, "I would like to tell you a parable, a story, to show you should never give up hope.

"There was once a cold-hearted judge," Jesus began, "who didn't love God and had little or no respect for the people of his village. What he really loved was his position of authority. A poor widow came to him one day and told him that she had lost what little money she had. Someone had tricked her.

"The judge told her to go away, that he couldn't be bothered by her small troubles. But the widow didn't give up. She came to the judge again and again, insisting that he do something to help her.

"Finally, the judge really got annoyed. He realized that the only way to get rid of the widow was to give her what she wanted. 'That woman is going to wear me out one of these days,' he thought. 'So I'd better do as she asks and have it over and done.' He called in the man who had taken her money and made him pay it back."

Jesus let his eyes rove over the eager faces of his apostles. "Learn from the parable of the judge," he said. "He did what the woman demanded because she asked often and would not be discouraged. I say to you that God, Who is just and kind, will hear your cries. Pray often, pray earnestly, and God will hear your prayers."

Because they were so close to Jesus in spirit, the apostles understood that there were right and wrong ways to pray. But, from time to time, when Jesus talked to the crowds about how they should pray, a few would shrug and turn away. Perhaps they thought they were better than the others. Or perhaps they had prayed so much, for so long, they thought they had nothing to learn.

One day, Jesus appeared to be talking to all those gathered before him. His words, however, were really directed to only a few who stood at the edge of the crowd, looking proud and keeping their distance from the rest.

"I'd like to tell you a parable now about two people who went into the temple to pray," Jesus said. "One was a Pharisee and the other a poor tax collector.

"The Pharisee, very sure of himself, stood in a place where the light would shine right on him. Lifting his face upwards, he bragged loudly, 'I thank You, God, that I am not like many others. I'm neither greedy nor dishonest nor unjust. And I'm certainly not like this tax collector here near me. Twice a week I do not eat. I fast, as everyone knows. And I contribute to the temple one-tenth of everything I make.'

"The tax collector was meanwhile hovering in the shadows, so humble he wouldn't even lift his eyes towards heaven. The man stood with his head bowed, hitting his fist against his chest, mumbling, 'God be merciful to me. I am a sinner.' "

Jesus did not need to look at the proud few at the edge of the crowd. He knew he had their attention. He went on:

"Do you know who was blessed by his prayers in the temple? The tax collector. God hears the people who are humble. He helps them, but He's not impressed by people who brag."

As Jesus and the apostles came closer and closer to Bethany, preaching to the crowds, Martha was busier than ever. She was an energetic housekeeper. Her house was big, bigger than most in the village, and every room had to be swept. And, of course, she had to see that the servants brought water from the well and prepared lots of food. The servants had to be watched to make sure they did everything correctly, and some things Martha felt only she could do herself.

Mary, on the other hand, did not make household chores her main concern. While she liked things nice and clean, from the first time she had met Jesus, a new purity seemed to have come over her. She had become dreamy. She was content to sit for hour after hour, recalling Jesus' words. The rest of the world simply did not exist for her.

Now that he was coming back again to their house, a sort of glow seemed to surround her. She was happy and yet, deep inside, she was troubled. She wanted to do something special for Jesus, something to show her respect for the Son of God.

One evening after Jesus and the apostles had arrived, they were all to dine at the home of a man named Simon. The meal went as planned, with simple, yet nourishing food and interesting conversation. After the meal was over, Mary quietly left the room. In a few moments she came back, looking serious. She was carrying a white marble jar of expensive oil. The fragrance was so pure and rich it filled the room. The oil was so costly, it was used only to prepare bodies for burial or to be touched to the forehead of kings, to show honor to them.

Mary went directly to Jesus, where she knelt and removed one of his sandals. Then, to the astonishment of the onlookers, she bathed one of his feet with the expensive oil. And then, Mary did another surprising thing. She raised her slim young arms to her head and loosened her hair. The thick, dark fullness of her hair fell down over her shoulders, almost to her waist. And then Mary, with eyes lowered and an almost saintly glow upon her face, bent her head forward. Taking a portion of her hair, she gently wiped the foot of Jesus. Then she repeated the process with Jesus' other foot.

The onlookers were stunned into silence at the sight of this young woman's devotion. But as Mary finished and leaned back on her heels, she became aware of murmurings from one corner of the room. Slowly, she turned to see the apostle Judas Iscariot striding towards her.

"Well, that was a pretty scene," he said with a scowl.

"But do I need to point out what a waste of money it was? That oil is worth a small fortune." His eyes blazed at Mary. "Since you are—or pretend to be—such a sweet, generous woman," he said, "why didn't you sell that oil and then give the money to the poor, where it would have done some good?" Mary shrank back from the words, noticing that the other apostles were also displeased. She looked toward Jesus as though asking if she had been wrong.

"Let her alone," Jesus said to Judas. "She has done a beautiful thing." And then, almost as though speaking to himself, he said, "You will always have the poor with you, and you can always do good for them. But you won't always have me." Judas turned on his heel and left.

Jesus touched Mary's shoulder. "You have prepared my body for burial before my death," he said. "For this, Mary, you will always be remembered."

Gradually, the talk began again and the rest of the evening passed quietly. If anyone noticed that Judas Iscariot had left so quickly, they did not seem to be concerned.

Judas, the treasurer for the apostles, was angry. How stupid of Mary, he thought, to toss away lots of money, money he could have used for better things than bathing someone's feet! If he had just guessed what she was up to before that little scene happened, maybe he could have taken Mary aside and talked her out of the oil.

She was a generous person, Judas knew. She could not have resisted his pleas for the poor people. Judas clutched the money bag hanging from his belt. Almost empty. Why did Mary waste all that money? And why did Jesus let her?

As he made his way down the winding streets, empty now in the darkness, Judas got even angrier. The money bag had to be fuller. Jesus had said they should not worry about money and clothes and other earthly possessions. The people should be like the lilies of the field and the birds in the sky. God would provide for them. But this evening had been too much. Money, right down the drain. Then, to top it all off, Jesus had actually taken Mary's side, even though Judas had spoken for other apostles, too.

Well, this whole business of following Jesus and pretending to go along with his ideas was going to stop. Jesus preached that the people should not be hypocrites, putting on a show. Judas no longer wanted to follow Jesus, and he would no longer pretend that he did.

Besides, there was talk going on. People were saying that Jesus was dangerous. For a while he had been just a harmless preacher, but now he had such a big following. He was too powerful. It was time to stop him.

Judas knew the Pharisees and high priests were talking openly against Jesus, and maybe with good reason. They had the citizens to think about. If Jesus got too powerful the Romans would step in, and, then, watch out!

His mind made up, Judas made his way to where the high priests had gathered for the evening. He came to the huge doorway and looked inside. The long room was dimly lighted except for lanterns flickering around a table in the back of the room, where the high priests were holding council. He paused only for a moment and then stepped through the doorway. The high priests turned and called out, "Who is there?"

Judas walked towards them. "It is Judas Iscariot."

The priests looked at one another, surprised. "What do you want?" one of them asked.

"I have come to give you some information," Judas said, without a pause. "I know where the man Jesus is, and what you must do to capture him." A look of cunning came over his face. "But, of course, I expect a reward for my trouble." His hand touched the small money bag at his waist.

The high priests eyed Judas. Then, carefully, one of them said, "And what is your price?"

Greed came into Judas' eyes. "Thirty pieces of silver."

"I could buy a slave for that price," one priest murmured, with a glance at the others. They looked at this traitor with interest, but they did not like him for what he was doing.

Judas clenched his fists. "Well?"

The leader motioned to one of the others. "Pay him," he said. Slowly, the priest withdrew a pouch and counted out thirty pieces of silver.

The coins glistened in the lamplight as the priest counted them, one by one. Judas' eyes glistened as the pile of money grew. A hand pushed the column of silver towards him. He snatched at the coins, clanking them into his leather pouch. He licked his lips, pulled back, and, with one hand pressing the pouch close to his body, said, "I'll point him out whenever you're ready."

And, as the priests watched, Judas turned and hurried out into the darkness. There, he leaned against the building. He began to shake. A terrible taste came into his mouth. What was it from? Fear? Shame?

What—have—I—done? he thought. What have I done, so quickly, and without planning? His mind whirled a little, but then he forced himself to concentrate on the facts. Everyone knew that Jesus' teaching could not go on much longer. Jesus himself was telling his followers that his days on earth were numbered. His life was bound to come to an end sooner or later. Judas was just helping things along.

He wiped his hand across his mouth and went on his way. The bag of silver at his waist felt like lead. But when he tried to ease the weight in his hands, the coins, cold and lifeless, felt warm—warm as blood—through the leather. Judas knew that this was just his mind playing tricks. Why shouldn't he, like anyone else, profit now and then? He had just done what any sensible man would have done.

Hadn't he?

Palm Sunday

Jesus had a faraway look in his eyes. The six days of sweet rest and good talk with his friends at Bethany were coming to a close. It was time to go to Jerusalem. There, Jesus knew he would die soon. But he was calm.

The apostles, on the other hand, were nervous and full of bad news. "I have just come back from the market place," Simon told Jesus. "There are some troublemakers around there. They're saying that you have too much power and too many followers. We have the feeling that there's a plot brewing against you, Master."

Jesus gazed fondly at Simon and the other apostles. He was like a father, trying to quiet the fears of his children. Yet, he was far apart from the apostles, too. All these months he had tried to make them ready for his death. No matter how much he had comforted them, though, they were still afraid and wanted to protect him.

"My dear friends," he said, "thank you for your concern. But can't you accept that my life must end soon? Haven't I told you so often enough?"

The apostles shrugged uncomfortably. Now John said, "All the same, I still wish you wouldn't go to Jerusalem. That's where all the trouble is. The Pharisees, the religious leaders, there are out to get you."

"I am not afraid of the Pharisees or of anyone who might be with them," Jesus said. "We will go to Jerusalem as planned to celebrate the holy feast of the Passover. What will be, will be."

Before Jesus left Bethany, he talked to his friends Mary,

Martha, and Lazarus. As they gathered around him outside the house, he told them not to be afraid. They must have faith, he said, no matter what happened to him. "Remember the words I have spoken," Jesus told them, "and live according to them. If you do, you will have everlasting life."

Mary clutched at the sleeve of Jesus' robe. "Don't leave, Master. I am afraid."

"Don't be afraid, Mary," Jesus told her. "I will always be with you." He made a little motion to Mary's sister Martha. She gently took Mary by the arm and led her to the house.

Now Jesus turned to Lazarus, whom he had raised from the dead only a short while ago. Jesus said, "It would be better for you to stay here, Lazarus, with your sisters. Your life is in danger because you are my friend. Do not come with me."

Lazarus bowed his head and answered, "I will do as you say."

Jesus walked away from the house. With his apostles and a few followers, he took the path that led to Jerusalem. Lazarus, squinting, watched until the group was out of sight. Jesus' last visit to Lazarus' house was over. Sadly, Lazarus joined his sisters.

The road to Jerusalem passed over the Mount of Olives. As Jesus and his followers walked the steep path that clung to the mountainside, he called two of his apostles close.

"See that village?" he said, pointing to a cluster of buildings nearby. "Go there. You will find a donkey with her colt. Their owner has tied them up, but they are not meant to remain there. They are meant to come here. I want you to untie them both and bring them back to me."

"But the owner may stop us. He will think we are thieves," said one apostle.

"Do not worry," answered Jesus. "If anyone says anything to you about taking the animals, just answer that the

Lord needs them right now. Say that He will send them back soon."

The two apostles did exactly as Jesus had said. They climbed down the mount and onto a grassy path that led to the village. Once there, they found the donkey and her colt, just as Jesus had said they would.

Perhaps the apostles were nervous. Supposing the owner rushed out at them, asking them what they thought they were doing, taking the animals? But the owner did nothing of the sort. No one tried to stop the apostles. No one interfered.

Soon they were back on the Mount of Olives with Jesus. When he saw the colt, he walked up to the frisky animal and calmed it with the soothing palm of his gentle hand. "This is the colt I shall ride, right into Jerusalem."

"But, Lord, that is such a lowly animal," a follower said, "the baby of a donkey."

"You ought to enter the city in a grand way," another follower suggested. "Why not take a chariot in? Show Jerusalem that you are a king. Ride in style, Jesus."

But the master shook his head. "No, I don't wish to go to Jerusalem as a warrior in a chariot. I do not wish to look like a messiah who has come to conquer. I wish to enter the city as a man of peace."

The apostles nodded in agreement. Several took off their outer robes and draped them over the colt's back. The cloth would make the ride down the hilly slopes of the Mount of Olives more comfortable for their master.

From here, Jesus began to ride the colt to the city. The apostles walked near him, and others followed around and behind them. As the little bunch moved along, other people, seeing Jesus, left what they were doing and joined in. Soon, the growing group ran into some travelers who were making their way to Jerusalem to celebrate the Passover. The travelers fell behind the people around Jesus and began to walk with him, too. In this way, the little bunch of people soon became a small crowd.

Then word began to spread that something unusual was going on. People began to stream from their homes. They stood along Jesus' path to watch him. The small crowd of people had become a large crowd now. And it was getting even bigger. Jesus was traveling more and more slowly, there were so many people in his path.

There was excitement in the air. "Who is this man?" some of those watching in the crowd shouted out.

"He is Jesus, the teacher from Nazareth," came a reply.

Soon the crowd was close enough to Jerusalem for the people there to see Jesus approaching with his followers. And people from the city rushed out to meet him, too. Then, a young person in the crowd whipped off his outer robe and spread it in Jesus' path. As though that had been a signal, other followers did the same with their outer robes. Soon, Jesus' colt was no longer walking on rough, uneven stones. The road had become soft: a carpet of the people's clothing.

Then someone else had a different idea. He began cutting branches from palm trees and laying them in Jesus' path. Other people did the same. Now the carpet before Jesus was green and thick with life and love.

The crowd continued to move toward Jerusalem, even more slowly now. Jesus often paused to speak to those pressing near him. Suddenly a young woman, with her small child in her arms, managed to get right up to the side of the colt. Swiftly, she lifted the child up into Jesus' arms. Then other parents, carrying their children or leading them by little hands, moved forward. Soon the young ones surrounded Jesus, looking at him with big smiles.

"Bless my child," one parent called out, hopefully. "Say a prayer over the head of my sweet young one."

Some of the apostles tried to direct the crowd away from

Jesus so that his path could be cleared and he could move forward. But Jesus, who wanted to be with the children, only drew them more closely to him. He put down the child resting in his arms only to pick up another who reached out for the master.

Jesus loved the children tenderly, and he wished them to come near him whenever they wanted to. He had once said that the Kingdom of Heaven belonged to the children and that grown-ups should be more like them. God, Jesus had said, loved the little ones very much. He wanted them all with Him in heaven.

The crowd of people moved forward a little more. Jesus still led the way on his colt. The people following him spread more and more palm leaves in his path. In time, the people would call this day Palm Sunday, there were so many of the plants carpeting Jesus' path.

There were not just children and parents in the crowd, of course. Jesus heard cries coming from others, too. "Out of the way, let us through," a voice shouted from one side. Two men came, carrying someone on a cot. The person on the cot was too sick to walk. Still, she wanted to follow Jesus, trusting that Jesus could heal her.

Cries rang out from many sick people: "Touch me!" "Heal me." "Heal my child." And Jesus spoke words of comfort to the sick people.

Now the crowd was very close to Jerusalem. By this time, there were so many people following Jesus, it was almost impossible for him to move. And they had begun to throw flowers in his path. The fragrance filled the air.

Some people from the city, drawn to the streets by the noise and commotion, asked, "What is going on here?"

Others told them, "See that man in white over there, riding the colt? That is Jesus, the teacher from Nazareth."

"Oh, really?" And their necks craned to get a better look.

"Isn't this the teacher that our leaders are trying to stop?" one Pharisee asked another. "They say he has too much freedom. Yet, today, I notice no one is trying to stop him from coming into Jerusalem. Just look at how the people adore him."

The other Pharisee lowered his voice to answer. "All in good time," he said. "What you are seeing today is a good example of how this Jesus sways the crowd. Just look at that mob. Believe me, this sort of thing won't continue for long. This Jesus has taken on too much power. And, as you know, power is a dangerous thing." The Pharisee now lowered his voice even more. "His days are numbered, believe me."

Jesus finally arrived at the temple in Jerusalem. He got off his colt, walked up the steps, and went inside the holy building. But, instead of finding a quiet place of worship, Jesus saw a noisy market. People were buying and selling

birds and animals, right in the temple. Cages creaked as the creatures inside tried to get out. Feathers flew in the air, floating down to the temple floor. Straw littered his path as Jesus walked through the hall.

Near the cages of animals were tables. Here, there were stacks of coins piled high in front of workers called money changers. They were arranging for the sale of the animals for sacrifice.

The time had come for Jesus to change the temple back to how it should be. It was no place to be making business deals and trading. It was no place for squawking animals, either.

Jesus, furious, stopped at a table filled with stacks of coins. Using both hands, he tipped the table over. Coins flew across the room. Then Jesus went swiftly to the cages and unloosed the birds and animals. There was a great commotion. Birds flew about, terrified. Animals scurried. Coins clattered. The sellers and money changers, meantime, were scrambling around, trying to gather up what belonged to them and get out of there. Jesus shouted to them, "It is written that God's temple is a house of prayer. But you have made it into a den of thieves."

With a whip, Jesus now began chasing the animals out of the temple. The sellers and money changers hurried even faster. Cringing, they finally ran off. At last, the temple was quiet and peaceful.

Now, slowly, softly from the shadows, the sick came up to the teacher from Nazareth. "Oh, put your hands upon us," they almost whispered, "so that we can be well."

Jesus, standing in the house of his Father, looked at these sick people with pity. Lovingly, he moved among them and cured them.

Then some children of the temple came forward. These were young boys who were training to become priests themselves one day. They had been standing, amazed, watching Jesus clear the temple and cure the sick. At first, the children had not been able to believe their eyes. Then, as they took courage and came close to Jesus, one voice cried out, "Hosanna!" And soon all the pure young voices called out, shouting with joy, "Be praised, Son of David."

But there were some religious leaders who had also been huddling together in the temple. Now they came forward, too.

"This is too much," one said to Jesus in a voice shaking with anger. "Isn't it bad enough that you preach to the grown-ups, giving them false ideas about God? Now you're misleading all of these young boys, too."

"Yes, I hear them," Jesus said. "From their young mouths comes the most perfect praise."

With one last look around, Jesus turned and left the temple.

The Last Supper

Peter and John waited beside the Pool of Siloam in Jerusalem. They watched as woman after woman came to draw water, place her jar on her head, and walk gracefully away. Not a breath of air stirred that warm spring day. Peter knelt down and helped himself to a handful of the cool, clear water.

"There he is," called John in an excited whisper. "There is the man with the water jar."

"You're right, John. It's just as Jesus told us. He said we'd see a man with a water jar, and here he comes."

"He must be the one we are to follow. He will lead us to the house where we are to prepare the Passover Feast."

The man filled the jar, turned, and walked up the hill. Staying some distance behind, the apostles followed.

Shops lined the crowded, narrow street. The shop owners hoped to sell goods to the thousands of visitors who had come to Jerusalem for Passover. The midafternoon air was heavy with the mixed smells of sweating animals and cooking odors from kitchens preparing food for the feast.

"Are we being followed?" cautioned Peter. "Look in back of you. Be sure the temple guards are not on our trail. We must protect Jesus. We must not let anyone know where we will celebrate Passover."

The two apostles walked slowly. They were going up Mount Zion. It was a hard climb. Each step they took scattered dust like a small cloud as they walked on the unswept cobblestone pavement. Sand ground into their sandaled feet.

Soon, the man they were following gave a quick glance to make sure the two apostles were still with him. He fumbled for a moment with the latch at the door of a large two-story house. Then he entered, leaving the door slightly open. "This must be the place," said Peter.

Casually, so as not to attract attention, they slipped inside the house, closing the door quickly behind them. "What do you want?" came a voice from the shadows.

"The Teacher says to you, 'Where is the guest room where I am to eat the Passover with my apostles?' " These were the passwords Jesus had given John.

With that, their host lighted a lamp. "Welcome!" he said. "You must be Jesus' apostles. Follow me." And he took them up an outside staircase to a large guest room. There, Peter and John prepared for the feast.

Soon, Jesus and the other ten apostles arrived. All thirteen men gathered in that upstairs room. Thomas bolted the door carefully to be sure they would be alone. The apostles huddled together. In a low voice, Matthew asked, "Do you think anyone knows we are here?"

Another apostle answered, "Not a chance. John and Peter were careful as they made the preparations. I don't think anyone except the man who owns this house has any idea where we are. Our lord is safe."

"What do you think? Is the master going to set up his kingdom tonight?" whispered Bartholomew to the group. "This night seems so special to Jesus."

"Yes, that must be it. Probably tonight or tomorrow he is going to let himself be crowned king."

The apostles were speaking softly. They did not want to disturb Jesus, who was alone in another part of the room. Their master seemed thoughtful and sad.

"Remember how it was on Sunday?" the whispered talk continued. "Everybody was cheering Jesus when he came riding into Jerusalem on his donkey colt. And all those children sang to him and threw flowers and palm branches into his path! What a day!"

"Yes, the people have finally recognized who he is. He must be ready now to claim his throne. Our own Jesus will be King of the Jews!"

"Take it easy, Matthew. There's not a way in the world he could set up a kingdom," protested Thomas. "The temple guards are ready to arrest him at any moment.

"His enemies, you know," continued Thomas, "have been trying to find some way to trap him for months. What Jesus did in the temple when he arrived in Jerusalem was the last straw. Jesus went to the temple to worship—and what did he find? A place of business! His driving the animals out with a whip and upsetting the tables of the money changers were too much for the temple leaders. Since then, Jesus has been in more danger than ever before. We must keep him out of sight, or the guards will surely arrest him."

"They'd never do it," replied Andrew. "The crowds wouldn't let them."

"Oh, the guards could do it, all right. They could arrest him at night, when the people weren't looking."

"But they'd never find him. The twelve of us would see to that!" Emotional Peter was always ready to declare his loyalty to Jesus.

"Pilate's soldiers are after him, too, remember," cautioned Thomas.

"Oh, we'll take care of them," Simon whispered.

The youngest apostle, John, could not agree with the violence Simon was hinting at. "Come on, Simon. That's not what we've heard Jesus teach these three years we've been together," John said. "I think he's got a different way of bringing about his kingdom. Remember, he said 'Love your enemies.' "

"But," replied Peter, "he is setting up his kingdom,

that's for sure. And he'll need all our help. He can count on me. I'm the one he calls his rock—I'm strong, steady, and dependable. I'll certainly have a place of highest honor in the new kingdom."

Peter glanced at Jesus. He recalled the time that the master had asked the apostles who they thought he was. Peter remembered that it had been he himself who had declared "You are the Christ, the Son of the Living God." Jesus had replied to him, "Blessed are you for what you have said. It is God Who has told you who I am." Then Jesus nicknamed him "the rock."

"Yes," thought Peter, "I am my master's rock. He knows he can depend on me."

"You're not his favorite, Peter. I am!" John's voice brought Peter's wandering thoughts back into the upper room. "He's going to have me sit next to him at the supper table tonight."

"We'll see who's going to be number one. Why, everyone knows it's me," boasted Simon. "I'm the one he can stand behind if the going gets rough."

Jesus moved to the small window and looked out over the city. He seemed unaware of the conversation that was going on in the room.

"Judas is the one Jesus made treasurer," Matthew proposed. He may be prime minister of Jesus' new kingdom."

"Don't be too sure of that," protested Thomas, who always had his doubts. "I don't think Judas is really honest with our money. I, for one, don't trust Judas. Look at him right now. He is sitting over there all by himself, fiddling with his money bag. He surely looks like he has something on his mind tonight. I wonder what it is.

"But enough of this. Let's get on with our supper."

The apostles' feet were hot and dirty. All day long they had walked the dusty streets of Jerusalem in only simple sandals. It was the custom to wash the feet before any feast.

In rich homes, a servant did the washing at the door of the house as everyone came in. But who would wash the apostles' feet before this special Passover meal? They certainly had no money to hire a servant. And each apostle thought that he was too good for the job, anyway. Not one of the twelve was willing to do a servant's work.

As they sat down to supper, the group continued their argument as to who would be greatest in Jesus' kingdom. Then, quietly, one of the men at the table got up. He went to a corner. There he took off his outer robe, tied a towel around his waist, and from a pitcher poured a bowl of water. The silent figure went to each of the apostles and washed his dirt-covered feet. Who was it? Which of the thirteen men had become a servant?

It was Jesus himself.

When Jesus had taken his place again at the head of the table, he said, "To be the greatest among people, you must be a servant to all people."

Shamed into silence, the apostles ate their dinner quietly. They listened closely as John and Jesus began the ceremony that was always a part of the Passover.

On the table before them was some lamb roasted with bitter herbs, a basket of unleavened—or flat—bread, some parsley, and a bowl of salt water. Also there was a paste called *charosheth*. The paste was a mixture of apples, raisins, nuts, and cinnamon. All these things were symbols of the suffering of the Hebrews when, centuries before, they had been slaves in Egypt. It was there that, obeying God, Moses had rescued the Hebrews and led them into the wilderness.

According to tradition, the youngest at the table was to ask a special question. The Apostle John was the youngest at this supper, so he raised his voice:

"Why is this night different from all other nights? Why do we have this dinner?"

Jesus was the one who answered, taking the role he had seen Joseph, his earthly father, take so many times. Jesus described the meaning of the Passover for the apostles seated around him:

"At Passover," he said, "we celebrate freedom. We remember the land of Egypt, and how the Hebrews were slaves there. We eat the charosheth, which represents the red clay from which our fathers, in the hot African sun, made bricks for Pharaoh's buildings. The bread has no yeast in it because, once freed, our ancestors left Egypt in such a hurry that their bread never had time to rise.

"And, we remember how God rescued them. We remember how Moses brought ten plagues upon Egypt. The tenth plague would cause the firstborn child of every household to die. But God told Moses how the firstborn of the Hebrew families could be saved. He said for the families to sacrifice lambs, and then to sprinkle their blood on the doorpost of every Hebrew home. If this was done, the firstborn in that home would not die. Death would pass over that house.

"This is why we eat roasted lamb at this Passover Feast. It reminds us that God saved the Hebrew children from the plague of death when they sacrificed lambs to Him."

Jesus paused as he glanced at the cup of the blood-red wine on the table before him. He picked up a piece of parsley and dipped it in the bowl of salt water. Another hand was in the dish along with his own. It was the hand of Judas.

"This parsley represents the branch the Hebrews used to sprinkle the blood of the sacrificial lamb on their doorposts. And the parsley's bitter taste also reminds us of their bitter pain. The salt water stands for their tears." He handed his parsley to Judas.

Jesus picked up some of the unleavened bread, broke it, and said a prayer of thanksgiving. "This is my body," he

said, "broken for you. When you eat this bread, remember me." The apostles broke off pieces of the bread, ate bites of it, and passed the bread along to one another.

Then Jesus took a goblet of red wine. "This cup of wine," he continued, "is a new agreement, or covenant, in my blood. When you drink this wine, remember me. For as often as you eat this bread and drink this wine, you declare the Lord's death until he returns." He passed the cup. Each apostle drank from it.

"God made a covenant with our ancestors. He gave them freedom and made the Hebrew slaves in Egypt His own people. They, in turn, promised to live as the People of God. This supper is to remind us of that first covenant.

"Now, with my death, there is to be a new covenant. God is going to rescue His people in a new way." Jesus rose to his feet.

"I will not eat bread or drink wine again until I eat and drink with you in the kingdom."

There was confusion at the table. "See," whispered Andrew, "he is proclaiming his kingdom tonight. I told you he would. If he won't eat or drink until his kingdom comes, he is bound to be crowned soon."

"But what about his death?" questioned Thomas. "He has told us again and again he will not remain on earth for long. How can he set up a kingdom?"

"Tomorrow," Jesus continued, "I will die. And one of you is going to betray me. It will be one of you who has eaten this Last Supper with me—one of you who has dipped his hand into the dish with me."

This the apostles would not believe. They rose from their places and crowded around him. They all began to speak at once. "It can't be! None of us would ever betray you." Each apostle in turn denied that he would betray Jesus.

"I'll stand by you," said Peter firmly. "I'll never let you down. Remember, Lord, I'm your rock. I'll go to prison with you—and even to death." Peter fingered the dagger beneath his robe. He would save his master.

"Peter, Peter," pleaded Jesus, pointing out the window. "You will not protect me. Before the first rooster crows at dawn tomorrow, you will three times have said that you don't even know me."

The Passover Feast was ending. Bewildered, the apostles did not know whether to be full of hope for Jesus' new kingdom or full of fear for his safety. The group sang together a great hymn of the Hebrew faith:

> "Oh give thanks to the God of Heaven,
> For His steadfast love endures forever."

Hardly anyone noticed that Judas had slipped silently out into the night.

Gethsemane: Soldiers arrest Jesus

Judas crept quietly down the stairs and out of the house. "I don't think Jesus or the other apostles saw me leave the supper table," he said to himself.

It had been a different Passover Feast—different from any he had ever attended before. Jesus had talked about it as though it was his last meal—his very last supper.

The dark night closed in around Judas as he rushed down the cobblestoned street. Heavy clouds covered the full Passover moon. Different thoughts battled in Judas' mind.

"I had such high hopes," he sighed to himself. "Three years ago when Jesus called me to be one of his apostles, I was sure that he was God's promised Messiah. I hate those Roman rulers that govern the Jews. With our own king—our Messiah—we could be free. When I first saw Jesus, I thought he might be the Messiah we need so badly to come. Jesus spoke of the Kingdom of God over and over again. He taught us a prayer that had in it the words 'thy kingdom come.' I believed, surely Jesus was the promised king who would rule the kingdom talked about in that prayer."

"But in these three years that I have been with him, all he has done is talk. I want action. I want to see God's Kingdom really come, now."

Judas stopped to throw a stone into a pool he was passing. "I want to see Rome overthrown. Jesus could deliver us from the Roman dogs that have taken over our country, if he would just go ahead and do it. On Sunday, anyone could see that the crowd was on his side. Everybody in Jerusalem, it seemed, was shouting 'Hosanna to the king' as Jesus rode his donkey colt through the city gate."

Judas stared at the round ripples his rock had made when he had thrown it into the pool. "Jesus talked tonight at supper as if he was going to die. I know his enemies want to get rid of him. But maybe he won't be killed.

"Well, one thing is for sure now. He'll be arrested. The deal I worked out with Caiaphas and the other high priests will take care of that. They gave me thirty pieces of silver to point Jesus out to them.

"The high priests are scared that the crowd won't let them arrest Jesus during the day. So, I will show them where he has been going to pray every night this week. I will take them to the Garden of Gethsemane. They can arrest him there.

"An arrest, of course, doesn't necessarily mean an execution. Maybe being arrested will really help Jesus' cause. Maybe it will force him to say openly that he is the Messiah and that his new kingdom is soon to begin. If things work out that way, maybe he'll thank me for the deal I made with the high priests. Maybe he'll thank me for having him arrested.

"I wonder if he suspects what I am doing. And I wonder what is going to happen in the Garden of Gethsemane. And later. Well, whatever happens is not my fault," Judas said, kicking another stone into the pool. Then he started again along the street to the high priest's house, to Caiaphas.

Malchus, Caiaphas' trusted servant, was standing by the house's gate. He held his lantern high as he watched each person who went by. Judas turned in at the gate. "Are you Judas Iscariot?" muttered Malchus in a hoarse whisper.

"Yes, I am Judas."

"Then come with me."

Judas followed the servant into the high priest's courtyard. There he found a large crowd. He could tell from the robes they wore that there were among them some of the most important people in all Palestine. He noticed many religious leaders—Pharisees and Sadducees—as well as a number of wise and learned men—the elders and the scribes. Armed temple guards were there, too, and Roman soldiers.

"Here is Judas," the servant Malchus said to his master Caiaphas as he brought the apostle forward.

"Ah, yes, Judas. We are glad to see you again," said Caiaphas. "We have waited for this moment with great excitement. We are glad you took our offer of thirty pieces of silver to show us where we could find Jesus. Now, we want you to take us to him tonight."

After the Last Supper had ended, Jesus had gone to a lovely garden at the foot of the Mount of Olives. Here, he often had come to pray. The peaceful Garden of Gethsemane was a good place for him to pray on this troubled night, too.

There was not much else left that Jesus could do. What choice did he have? He had seen Judas leave the Passover Feast before anyone else had. Perhaps Judas was even now on his way to the high priest. Caiaphas would stop at nothing to have Jesus arrested, tried, and killed.

All of the apostles were with him except Judas. "Wait here and pray," he had told the eleven men. "Tonight I am going to pray apart from you. I want to talk with my heavenly Father alone."

Jesus had climbed farther up the Mount of Olives. Peter, James, and John, always trying to protect him, had followed a little behind. Jesus had knelt beneath a twisted olive tree. This is where he now prayed.

Jesus was troubled. His earthly world had begun to crumble. What had happened?

He knew his mission had been to bring God's Kingdom to earth. But where was that kingdom now? Where were the crowds that had followed him day by day in Galilee as he preached and taught and healed? Five thousand people had been with him on one occasion. As they had heard him preach, they had not wanted to leave, even to go home to eat. He had fed all of them with the food that one young boy gave him: two little fish and five loaves of bread. Some of Jesus' followers had wanted to crown him king then.

Where were those followers tonight?

And only four days before, Jesus had entered Jerusalem like a king, praised by the people. "Hail," they had shouted. "Hosanna to the king!"

Where were those people tonight?

Jesus rose from his knees and looked around him. The full moon came from behind a cloud. By its light, he could see Peter, James, and John, his three best friends. Jesus smiled sadly. The three apostles were supposed to be praying. But here they were—fast asleep instead.

Jesus' heart began to pound. He felt a loneliness he had never felt before. Even his closest friends were not helping him when he needed them the most. He knew that Judas had already made arrangements to betray him. Any moment Jesus' enemies could capture him. And he knew Peter, his most loyal apostle, was going to deny he had ever known him.

Throughout his teaching, Jesus had waited for the religious leaders to support his cause. But that had not happened. Instead, those leaders were now plotting his death.

If he were killed, he knew, he would be tortured to death on a cross. That was the Roman method of executing criminals and slaves. Jesus knew about crucifixions. He had seen them as he was growing up. When he was only a boy, two thousand men had died on crosses in Judea, in the country around Jerusalem. The crime of these men was that they had tried to free the Jewish people by overthrowing Rome. Sometimes, even now, his mind could still hear the screams of those dying men as they hung in the hot sun.

Had Jesus failed? The kingdom had not come. Tonight he would be arrested. Then a hearing would take place. Tomorrow, he would die on the cross. His work seemed a total failure.

He fell with his face to the ground and prayed. He was overcome by a sense of loneliness and failure. Was this sense of loneliness a part of the plan God had for him?

"If it is possible," he prayed to his Father, "let me not have to go through this suffering." Sweat poured from Jesus' forehead as if it was large drops of blood. "Father," he prayed again, "don't make me have to do this." The burden of the whole world rested on Jesus' shoulders.

As a boy, in the synagogue school in Nazareth, Jesus had memorized many passages from the holy writings. One of these passages came to mind now. Isaiah the prophet had written the words many centuries before. He had said that the Messiah was a suffering servant.

"He was wounded for our sins," Isaiah wrote, as though he had already seen the suffering. "He was beaten for our evil deeds like a lamb about to be killed. But the Messiah never said a word. He was arrested and sentenced and led to die. He was put to death for the sins of the people, and he willingly gave up his life. He took the place of many sinners and prayed that they might be forgiven."

Could it be? Was it possible that what was happening to Jesus now was really part of that ancient plan of God that Isaiah had written about? Maybe Jesus had not failed after all. Maybe the mission of the Son of God was different from what most people thought.

But Jesus was still afraid. "Lord," he prayed, "if it is

possible, let there be some other way. Please, God," he said, "I don't want to go through all this." Jesus' robe was wet with perspiration. His fingers clutched at the ground where he prayed. The Garden of Gethsemane filled with his great sobs.

"And yet, Lord, I will do Your will. It is not my own will but Yours that must be done."

Jesus pulled himself to his knees, then stood. He wiped the tears and sweat from his face with the sleeve of his already damp coat. Slowly, he walked to where he had left Peter, James, and John. They were still asleep.

"Could you not watch with me for one short hour?" he said to their closed eyes. "When I needed you most, you let me down. But wake up now. It is time to go."

As he was speaking, the Garden of Gethsemane became bright as daytime. The light was coming from torches and

lanterns. A mob, armed with swords and clubs, was marching up towards Jesus. Leading them was Judas—one of Jesus' own apostles.

"Hello, Master," said Judas. And he kissed Jesus on the cheek.

"That's the one," shouted Malchus, "the one Judas kissed. That was the sign that Judas was to use to give Jesus away. Arrest that man."

Two armed police and several Roman soldiers ran to seize Jesus. But the master simply walked toward them and looked at them. It was a look of sorrow, not fear.

"Let the men with me go. I'm the one you want," Jesus said. Then he asked calmly, "But why do you come to arrest me in the middle of the night? I've been in your temple every day. I'd have come with you then. What are you afraid of?"

Embarrassed, the guards fell back for an instant. It was the moment for which Peter had been waiting. He whipped a dagger from beneath his robe and lunged at Malchus. "You can't arrest our master," he shouted. He swung his knife as he charged. It hit Malchus on the head and cut off his ear.

"No more of this!" It was Jesus who gave the command. "I do not want you fighting others for me."

Jesus touched Malchus' ear. Suddenly, it was healed.

Malchus fell back, astonished. "This is no ordinary man we are arresting," he thought. "Who can this be?"

The guards tied Jesus' hands and began to lead him away. Confused and frightened, most of the apostles ran from the Garden of Gethsemane. Two of them, Peter and John, lingered behind, hiding in the shadows. They wanted to see what was going to happen.

Hoping not to be noticed, they followed their master as he was led away into the night.

A sentence of death for Jesus

It was midnight. There was hardly a sound in Jerusalem. Most of the people were asleep. But, in the courtyard of Caiaphas, the high priest, all was noise and confusion as a mob of people pushed their way in. Caiaphas himself stood in the courtyard, waiting.

"Here is the man you asked us to bring to you. They call him Jesus," the captain of the temple guards said. "We arrested him as you told us to do. Judas led us right to him and identified him with a kiss."

"You have done well. Bring the prisoner into my house. Already the members of the religious council are there. We want to begin this investigation into Jesus' activities right away." Caiaphas turned and walked toward the house.

"You heard the high priest, prisoner," shouted the captain at Jesus. "Move along!" He struck Jesus on the back with a heavy stick. Jesus did not say a word. Calmly, he walked up the stairs and entered a large room where the religious councilors were waiting for him. With them were some men who had come to report to the council on Jesus' activities. These men would serve as eyewitnesses for the investigation that was about to begin.

When the men began to give their reports, these reports did not seem to agree. Everyone at the hearing became confused, listening first to one version of something Jesus had done, and then listening to another version. One man reported: "I heard Jesus say that he was going to destroy the temple in three days and then build it again."

"And I heard him say the same thing," said another. But

Nicodemus, a councilor who knew Jesus, rose to his feet. "When was it that Jesus said he would destroy the temple?"

"He said that on Tuesday—just before sundown."

"But I was with Jesus myself at that time," Nicodemus said. "What I heard him say was that someday God would destroy the temple. That is an entirely different thing."

Another councilor, Joseph of Arimethea, rose to speak now. "I heard him, too. He said that God would destroy the temple. As to building something back in three days, that had nothing to do with the temple. One of Jesus' apostles told me it has to do with Jesus' body being destroyed and then raised again in three days."

Nicodemus spoke again now. "Tell me," he said to the eyewitness, "which did Jesus say: that God would destroy the temple or that Jesus would?"

"I thought Jesus said that he himself would."

Caiaphas began to look uneasy. The meeting was not working out as he had hoped it would. If they kept on at this rate, the investigation into Jesus' activities would stop right here. They would never get to have a formal hearing, and they certainly would never be able to bring Jesus before Pontius Pilate, the Roman governor, for trial.

Disgusted with the eyewitnesses, Caiaphas turned to Jesus himself. "What do you have to say about this report?" Jesus remained silent. "Come, come, prisoner. Speak up!" Caiaphas' face was turning red with impatience, but Jesus still did not speak. Caiaphas decided to try one last approach. "Jesus, some people claim that you are the Messiah. Tell us plainly, are you the Son of God?"

Now, for the first time, Jesus spoke: "Yes, I am."

"Well, we need no more evidence, then," said Caiaphas, relieved. "The prisoner claims to be the Son of God. That shows disrespect for the Lord. It is the crime of blasphemy. Councilors, what should we do with this man?"

Then the room was filled with cries of agreement. "This calls for a formal hearing. Take him to the temple. Let the judges there decide whether to take him to the Roman governor for a real trial."

Caiaphas spoke to the guard at the door. "Lead this prisoner away. We will follow. The moment daylight comes, the formal hearing will begin at the temple."

Meanwhile, in the courtyard below, Caiaphas' maid came to bring wine to the weary guards who waited there. She threw a new log on the fire. Soon, the fire burned more brightly. By its light, she caught a glimpse of a stranger who had sneaked in trying to see what would happen to Jesus. It was the Apostle Peter. "Look," she exclaimed. "That man over there in the shadows—I've seen him before. He is one of Jesus' apostles."

"You must be mistaken," replied Peter, frightened that the temple guards would arrest him, too, "I never saw that prisoner Jesus before in all my life."

Peter moved to the porch. But another maid saw him there and said to him, "I know who you are. You were with Jesus when the guards arrested him. You must be one of his apostles."

"Why do you accuse me of being the friend of a common criminal?" Peter swore, "I do not know the man."

"Come on, now," said one of the guards. "You can't fool us. Your accent—the way you talk—gives you away. You come from Galilee, just as Jesus does. You are one of his apostles. I am sure of it."

With that, Peter became angry. "I told you I don't know that man. I never saw him before in all my life."

Somewhere in the distance, the silence of the night was broken. A rooster crowed. Just at that moment, guards led Jesus through the courtyard. He turned to look at Peter. And Peter remembered the words Jesus had spoken to him at the Last Supper, just a few hours ago: "Before the first

rooster crows at dawn tomorrow, Peter, you will three times have said that you don't even know me."

Peter ran from the courtyard. He threw himself down beside the road and cried as if his heart would break.

Now, guarded and chained, Jesus walked toward the temple in Jerusalem. In a hall next to the temple, his formal hearing would take place. The crowd that had been at Caiaphas' house followed.

The formal hearing did not take long. It began the moment the sun began to rise. Seventy judges sat in a semicircle in the hall. Jesus stood before them.

Caiaphas, the high priest, questioned Jesus as he had earlier. But Jesus refused to answer. "You won't say anything?" said Caiaphas. "Well, no matter. These men heard you last night claiming to be the Son of God, the Messiah. That is blasphemy, a crime against God. Judges, what is your decision?"

"Death. Take him to the Romans for trial, so that they will execute him."

Caiaphas stood in the hall as the guards took Jesus away. The high priest was relieved that the Romans would take over now. But, just then, a man burst into the room and ran angrily up to Caiaphas. It was Judas Iscariot, the apostle who had betrayed Jesus.

"Take back your filthy money," Judas screamed. He threw the thirty pieces of silver, the money Caiaphas had paid him, at the high priest. "We both know Jesus is innocent of any crime. Now, because of us, he will die."

Then Judas stormed from the hall. With a rope in his hand, he began to climb a hill outside the city. Finally, he reached a cliff. There, he tied one end of the rope to a tree that grew over the cliff. The other end of the rope, Judas tied around his neck. Then the apostle stepped to the edge of the cliff. There, he hanged himself.

In the judgment hall, the Roman governor, Pontius Pilate, was frightened. He did not want to sentence Jesus. He thought about a warning his wife had given him, just that morning. She had had a dream about Jesus. She had said he was a good man and that Pilate must not have anything to do with harming him. But now, with Jesus before him in the hall, Pilate had no choice but to begin questioning him. "Are you the King of the Jews?" Pilate asked Jesus. He looked at the prisoner, who was calm in spite of the chains around his wrists.

"You yourself say it, not I," replied Jesus.

Pilate knew what he ought to do. He ought to release Jesus. The case had nothing to do with Rome. This was obviously a religious matter, not one for the Roman governor. "I do not find this man guilty of any crime," Pilate announced.

"But you can't release him," argued Caiaphas. "Jesus has stirred up trouble everywhere. He is too powerful to release, especially in his home region of Galilee."

"He is a Galilean?" Pilate asked, relieved. Now the Roman governor saw the way to escape having to sentence Jesus. "The ruler of Galilee, King Herod, is right here in the city, celebrating the Passover. Send Jesus to Herod to be judged. Herod is the ruler of Galilee, not me."

King Herod was pleased and excited by the news that Jesus was coming. The king had heard much about Jesus' miracles. He had heard that Jesus could make the lame walk and the blind see. There were even rumors that Jesus had turned water into wine. Herod wanted to see some miracles, too. "Let's have some fun with this prisoner," he said. "I understand he calls himself a king. Servants, bring my old purple robe and put it on him when he arrives, so that he looks like a king."

Now Jesus stood before Herod, who asked, "Are you a king, Jesus?" But Jesus did not answer Herod. "Are you the Son of God, Jesus?" Jesus was still silent. "Do you think you are King of the Jews?" Jesus said nothing. "Do some miracles for us." Jesus simply looked at Herod.

King Herod quickly ran out of patience. Jesus was not going to be any fun at all. "Send the prisoner back to Pilate," Herod commanded, angrily. "Let Pilate deal with this stubborn man." And still Jesus remained silent.

Now the crowd took Jesus back to Pilate, the Roman governor. But Pilate still wanted to free Jesus. "You have already brought me this man once," he said to the priests and leaders, "and you told me the charges you had against him. I have examined his case myself, and I do not find him guilty of breaking any law. Neither did Herod. He simply sent him back to me. Isn't that enough for you?

"Look, here is my offer," Pilate continued. "If he must be punished, then I will have the soldiers give him a good beating. Be satisfied with that. Then, as you know, at Passover I always release one of your people who is a prisoner. This year, I will release Jesus, after his whipping.

"Centurion," Pilate called to one of the Roman officers in the hall. "Take the prisoner and beat him."

The soldiers took off Jesus' purple cloak, which Herod had put on him, and chained him to a post. Then they beat his bare skin. Blow after blow tore his flesh to shreds. But even though each blow cut into him, only Jesus' face showed his pain. For Jesus never said a word.

After the beating, the soldiers put the purple robe back on Jesus. One of the soldiers made a crown out of a thorny vine. He jammed it on Jesus' head. The thorns cut into Jesus' forehead. He could feel large drops of blood streaming down his face. "Hail, King of the Jews!" a soldier laughed mockingly. "Let's see you govern us." The soldier hit Jesus on the head. The crown of thorns cut even more deeply. Another soldier knelt before Jesus, making fun of him.

"Oh, King, where is your kingdom?"

Jesus looked at the soldier with pity in his eyes, but he did not say a word.

When Jesus stood again before Pilate, the governor turned to the crowd and said, "See, I have punished your King of the Jews. He is bruised and bloody. See the man? Now I release him to you."

"No," the crowd shouted, "release another prisoner to us. Release Barabbas, the murderer and rebel. We want Jesus crucified instead of the murderer. Crucify Jesus. Crucify him. Crucify him!" the noisy crowd demanded.

"But I find no crime in him, I tell you. There is no reason to crucify this man."

The leaders of the Jews now answered Pilate: "We have a religious law, and by that law he ought to die. He has committed the crime of calling himself the Son of God. That is blasphemy."

Pilate turned to Jesus. "Where are you from?" Again, Jesus gave no answer. "Don't you know I have the power to release you or to crucify you?" Pilate could not understand the man who stood before him. How could he be so calm? Why didn't he defend himself?

An assistant to Pilate whispered to him, "Your wife sends a message, a warning to you. She says to remember her dream. Do not hurt this good man."

At this point, Pilate was ready to set Jesus free. But the crowd cried out, "If you let this man go free, you are no friend of Caesar, the Roman emperor. We will tell Caesar what you have done. Anyone who calls himself a king is a threat to the emperor."

Pilate trembled. He did not wish to displease Caesar. Finally, he made Jesus sit in the seat of judgment—Pilate's own seat. Jesus was still wearing Herod's kingly purple robe, and on his head he still wore the crown of thorns. Pilate, pointing to Jesus, said, "Here is your king. Shall I crucify your king?"

"We have no king but Caesar," the angry mob shouted. "Away with this prisoner who calls himself our king. Let him be crucified!"

Pilate called for a bowl of water. In front of all the crowd he washed his hands. "See," he said, "I am innocent of this whole affair. I am washing my hands of Jesus' blood and the guilt that goes with it."

Then Pilate released Barabbas, the prisoner who had been scheduled to die on the cross that same day. "We will crucify Jesus instead, if you must have it," Pilate said.

And again the soldiers played their cruel game. Even more of them gathered around Jesus to make fun of him. They hit him and beat him. They spit on him. They laughed at him. Then, finally, they took off the purple robe he was wearing and put his own cloak back on him.

And then they led Jesus away to be crucified.

The cross

The centurion sighed. He was one Roman army officer who hated his assignment. He had never wanted to come to Jerusalem in the first place. The people here were always making trouble. The Roman government had stationed him here with the Roman soldiers to try to keep order. And he knew that at any minute trouble might break out. Just a few days ago, for instance, there had been a riot led by a man named Barabbas, head of a gang of bandits.

"I put that one down," the centurion said to himself. "I had Barabbas thrown into prison. But today they've let him out of jail—even though he was scheduled for crucifixion. Now they have ordered me to crucify a man called Jesus."

The people of Palestine, the centurion knew, hated him and all the other Romans. The people seemed to be waiting for just the right leader to save them, to set them free. The centurion halfway sympathized with them. He did not want to be in Palestine any more than the Jews wanted him there. He wished he had never heard of this out-of-the-way Roman province. "Oh, to be back home in Rome," he sighed.

In Rome, he had led a pleasant life as a professional soldier. He had been surrounded by many of his boyhood companions. He could visit the Roman baths every day. And, at the arena, he could also watch the chariot races.

But here is Jerusalem there was nothing compared to the attractions of Rome. And now this assignment! Why did he have to be in charge of crucifixions on such a beautiful spring Friday?

There were three men to be nailed to crosses and left to die in the hot sun. Two of the men were thieves. One of them, however, was an innocent man called Jesus. Even Pontius Pilate, the governor, had not been able to find this man guilty of any crime. The centurion had attended the trial in the judgment hall early that morning. He had seen Pilate try again and again to set Jesus free. But finally Pilate had given in to the demands of the local political and religious leaders. He had ordered that Jesus be crucified.

"This prisoner Jesus," the centurion thought to himself, "doesn't seem at all like a criminal. When Pilate ordered the soldiers to beat Jesus, his skin was torn to shreds. But he never said a word. Every other condemned man I have seen beaten has cursed and sworn and screamed. But not this one. He's unusual. While I was standing there supervising the beating, he looked at me as though he felt sorry for me. Imagine that."

Crucifixions were nothing new to the soldier. As a centurion, a professional soldier with a hundred other soldiers under his command, he had been in charge of this type of execution many times. Crucifixion was an ugly method of death, used by the Romans only for the worst criminals.

But the centurion had no choice. He led the group of condemned men and officials through the narrow streets of Jerusalem and to the place of execution. It was called Calvary, "the Place of the Skull." Each condemned man was made to carry the heavy crossbar to which he would soon be nailed. Four soldiers formed a square around each prisoner. And someone carried a huge sign in front of each, telling what crime the condemned person had committed. Rome wanted people to see what happened to anyone who dared to break Rome's laws.

Jesus bent almost to the ground as he carried the heavy wooden beam to which he would be nailed. "Move along there, prisoner. You can go faster than that," shouted one of the soldiers. "We want to get this thing over with. Move!" With a whip he carried, the soldier gave Jesus a lash across the back.

Jesus' robe was stuck to dried blood on his body. The blood had come from the beating Jesus had already received earlier that morning. The heavy beam rubbed his sores open again and sent stinging pain all through his body. Jesus fell to the ground three times under the weight of the cross. "We'll never get to Calvary at this rate," growled a soldier.

"Hey, you there!" barked the centurion to a man on the street. "Carry this man's cross. We are in a hurry."

Simon of Cyrene had saved all his life to have the money to come to Jerusalem to celebrate the Passover. And now this. Instead of the joyful occasion he had expected, he had to carry a criminal's cross to a place of execution. It had been a long journey from Simon's home in Africa to Jerusalem. What a way to have it end. But Simon did as he was told. One did not refuse a centurion's command.

Two soldiers picked up the heavy wooden beam and dropped it with a thud across Simon's big shoulders. Jesus pulled himself to his knees and then to his feet. He looked at Simon with a gratitude that Simon would never forget. With the crossbar on his back, walking in front of Jesus, Simon for a while was part of the group going to the execution.

As the group climbed up the steep hill of Calvary, the centurion could see at the top three tall poles that had been driven into the ground. Jesus and two thieves were soon to be nailed to the crossbars they carried. The crossbars would then be pulled up and placed across the poles.

The centurion heard the last nails driven into the wrists of the prisoners. Then he watched the crossbars lifted into place. He settled down to wait for death to come to the condemned men.

He could not keep his eyes off the center cross, where Jesus hung. "This is Jesus, the King of the Jews," read the sign over his head. It was the same sign that had been carried in front of Jesus through the streets to let people know his crime. "A strange kind of crime," thought the centurion.

As four of the soldiers amused themselves by gambling for the clothes of the men on the crosses, the centurion took off his helmet to cool his head. He adjusted his shield beside him so he could sit in its shade. Then he took a long drink from his flask. Even though it was morning, the blistering sun made him quite uncomfortable. He shaded his eyes and tried to rest.

For some reason, however, he could not seem to relax. He kept thinking about the man on that center cross. Now Jesus was trying to say something. The centurion looked up and listened.

"Father, forgive them," Jesus was saying. "Forgive them, for they do not know what they are doing."

The centurion could not believe what he was hearing. How could a man who was being tortured to death pray that God would forgive the same people who had condemned him? "Can he really be asking God to forgive us?" wondered the amazed centurion.

Crucifixions always attracted a large crowd of curious people. Today was no exception. Some of the crowd who had called for this innocent man's crucifixion earlier that morning had followed him to Calvary. They seemed to enjoy the event immensely. As they watched, they laughed and joked.

"Hey, you there, on the center cross," one shouted. "If you are really the Son of God, why don't you just show us by coming down? Show us that you really are the Son of God, as you claim to be."

Laughter rang through the crowd. "See, I told you,"

scoffed another. "He saved others, but he can't save himself." The mob laughed again.

Jesus said nothing in reply.

Most of the soldiers were laughing, too. They looked at the sign above Jesus' head, the sign that read "King of the Jews."

"Some king you are," mocked the soldiers. "Who ever heard of a king dying on a cross?" The hillside echoed with the coarse laughter of the soldiers and the crowd.

Even one of the thieves who was on one cross beside Jesus joined in the jeering. "So you are the Christ—the Savior," he scoffed. "Go ahead. Save yourself—and us, too."

But the other thief somehow did not feel like making fun of the man who was dying beside him. He argued with his partner. "Aren't you afraid of God? This man who is dying between us has done no wrong. Yet, he has been condemned to death, just as we. After all, we are getting what we deserve. We are guilty—but he is innocent."

As best he could, the thief tried to turn his head toward Jesus. "Remember me," he pleaded. "Remember me, in your kingdom."

As the flies and gnats swarmed around his bleeding body, Jesus moved his thorn-crowned head toward the thief. There was a kingly sound to his voice. "Truly," said Jesus, "today you will be with me in Paradise."

The centurion wondered what all this could mean. He had never before witnessed a crucifixion like this one. From his cross, Jesus had spoken like a king. The centurion picked up his flask and took another sip.

Though it was daytime, the sky seemed to be getting darker and darker. The centurion mopped his brow with his cloak. Great clouds were blackening out the sun. Frightened by the strange darkness, the crowd became silent. Now the only sound was the sobbing of the few who had followed Jesus to the cross. These people loved him and believed in him. They cried in deep sorrow.

All that they had seen Jesus try to do seemed to have failed. Their hopes for God's new Kingdom had been so high only a few weeks before. And now they saw the one they had called Lord dying the death of a criminal. Through the blackness, the centurion heard Jesus almost crying, too. "My God," Jesus called, "my God, why have You forsaken me?"

"Your Kingdom of God never came," someone yelled. "And now you are all alone. Not even your God can help you now."

Everything seemed black as midnight. The centurion, who had been sweating a moment before, shivered.

As the time dragged by, it became difficult for Jesus even to speak. He was growing weaker, and his lips and throat were dry as sand. "I'm thirsty," he admitted.

One of the soldiers dipped a sponge into a jar of a drink that tasted like vinegar. Then, on a stick, the soldier lifted the sponge up to Jesus' lips.

Made anxious by the threatening sky, many who had come to jeer had now gone home. But several women and one or two men who loved Jesus were determined to stay until the end to help in any way they could.

Among the faithful women who had followed him to the cross, Jesus saw his own mother, Mary. He could not forget the love and care that she had given him throughout his life. He was concerned about what would become of her after his own death. He was her son, and he felt it his responsibility to care for her.

Only one of his apostles had had the courage to come to the cross. It was John—the one whom in many ways Jesus perhaps loved the most. Jesus looked at his mother and John as they stood near each other. He said to his mother, "Behold your son." And to John he said, "Behold your

mother." John understood. He put his arm around Mary. From that time on, John cared for her as though she were his own mother, too.

The centurion had seen Jesus take care of his mother, his one last duty. Now, the centurion heard Jesus' voice again, strong for the final moment. The innocent man gave what sounded almost like a cry of victory: "It is finished!"

Then these words followed: "Father, into Thy hands I commit my spirit." The centurion saw the thorn-crowned head go back in one last jerk of pain. Then it fell peacefully forward. Jesus had breathed his last.

The centurion did not know that these final words were part of a psalm, or holy poem, that Jesus had often recited as a child. Many Jewish mothers taught their children to say this psalm to God at bedtime, just before falling asleep each night. Jesus had died like a trusting child who was

going to sleep in the arms of a loving parent. With his last words, he had placed himself into the safekeeping of God.

As Jesus died, an earthquake shook the city of Jerusalem. Even the great curtain that hung in the middle of the temple was torn from the top to the bottom. Most of the crowd around the crosses fled. The soldiers shook with fear. What was happening? Darkness, an earthquake—what next?

But it was not the darkness and the earthquake that worried the centurion. It was the man he had been watching on that center cross. The centurion tried to pull himself together. He tried to understand what he had seen on Calvary that day. Was Jesus the Son of God after all?

The centurion moved to the foot of the center cross. He stood looking up into the face of the man whom he had helped to crucify. He remembered that this cross had been made for another criminal. As the centurion gazed up in silence, his mind heard again some of the jeers that had been hurled at Jesus that day.

"So you are the Christ," some had laughed.

"So you are the Savior!" others had jeered.

The sign still hung above Jesus' head: "This is Jesus, the King of the Jews."

The centurion had seen Jesus' agony. The weight of the sins of the world seemed to have rested on the dying man's shoulders. The centurion could almost hear Jesus' voice again, praying, "Father, forgive them, for they don't know what they are doing."

"He was praying for me, too," the centurion realized. "He was praying for me. This Jesus died like a king."

The centurion stood there in awe and wonder at what he had heard and seen that day. At last he turned to one of the other soldiers. He tried to put his thoughts into words. He whispered them to his companion: "Surely, this was the Son of God."

The Risen Christ

Jesus was dead. There was no doubt about that. A Roman soldier had stuck his spear into Jesus' side, to make sure.

At the foot of the cross, Nicodemus and Joseph of Arimathea stood, heads bowed. Mary, Jesus' mother, stood near them. She was pale, but her face remained lifted towards the cross. Jesus' agony was over. For this, Mary was glad.

It was time to take Jesus from the cross, to bury him. Nicodemus and Joseph of Arimathea lifted up their arms to receive the wilted body as it was dropped from the crossbar. Mary weakly reached out towards the lifeless body of her son. One woman who had stood with Mary through the cruel day now came near to comfort her.

Nicodemus said, "We must hurry. It will be sundown in a few minutes, and the Sabbath will begin. It is against the law to bury anyone on the Sabbath. We are lucky just to have permission to bury Jesus properly, you know."

"And it's a good thing the garden is so close, too," replied Joseph. "I have the tomb there all ready for Jesus."

Nicodemus and Joseph were both religious leaders of the Jews. During Jesus' lifetime, they had been able to admire him only in secret. But now, with his death, they had new courage. Perhaps it was because Jesus had died so quietly, without complaint. Perhaps it was because with Jesus' death, the Roman and Jewish officials would no longer find Jesus' followers dangerous. But, in any case, something about Jesus' death had given Nicodemus and Joseph courage.

They had boldly gone straight to Pontius Pilate, the Roman governor. They had received his permission to take Jesus' body down from the cross.

Nicodemus and Joseph were going to bury Jesus in a garden tomb. The tomb was like a cave, above the ground. Joseph had bought it for his own burial. But he was giving the tomb up so that Jesus would have a place to rest.

Two men, along with some women who loved Jesus, too, hurried to the tomb. There, they all worked quickly, preparing Jesus' body for burial. They tenderly wrapped him in long linen cloths, then placed the wrapped body inside the tomb. The women watched as strong men helped Nicodemus and Joseph roll a heavy stone across the opening to the cave.

Soon the tomb was not only closed, but also it was sealed and guarded. Political and religious leaders who had feared Jesus had gone to Pilate to make a request.

"Sir," they had said. "Give us soldiers to guard the tomb of Jesus of Nazareth, whom you crucified. We remember how he said, 'After three days I will rise again.' We suspect that his apostles might try to steal his body and then claim that Jesus has risen from the dead. There would be lots of trouble if the people thought Jesus had risen."

"Yes—yes, of course," said Pilate. "I will give you soldiers to seal the entrance to the grave and stay on guard night and day." The leaders thanked Pilate and went their way.

"That takes care of Jesus," gloated Caiaphas, the high priest, stroking his beard in satisfaction. "We saw him die—and now there is no possible way that his apostles or anyone else can get into the tomb to steal the body."

"Well," sneered a religious leader, a Pharisee, "I don't think we have much to worry about. That bunch of cowards ran away and hid the moment we arrested Jesus. They must be hiding still."

It seemed the apostles' entire world had crumbled around them. In their loneliness and despair, they had secretly gathered together in the same upstairs room where on Thursday night they had eaten the Last Supper with Jesus.

There was some comfort for them in just being together. Here in Jerusalem they were away from their own families, but they did have each other. Some of the men were sobbing in their grief and sorrow. Some just sat in silence.

The doors were locked. The apostles were grieved, of course, but they were also afraid. "None of us is safe," said James. "The temple guards are likely to arrest any of us if they find us. We may be crucified, too."

"The man who owns this house is a follower of Jesus. He was kind enough to say that we may stay here as long as we want," said Andrew, with gratitude in his voice.

The hours of the Saturday Sabbath dragged on. When it was over, the apostles tried to sleep. Just as a rooster crowed at dawn on Sunday, the apostles were awakened by a pounding on the door.

"It's the police," whispered Andrew.

"Open up. Open up!"

To their relief, the apostles realized that it was a woman who was shouting. "Open up, I have something to tell you. Open the door, quickly!"

"That sounds like either Salome or Joanna." Thomas fumbled with the latch on the door and finally got it open.

Several women burst into the room. Joanna and Salome led the group. With them also were two women, each named Mary. One was Mary, the mother of the Apostle James. The other was Mary Magdalene. Some other women followed behind, too.

Joanna spoke first. "His body is gone. The tomb is empty."

"At daybreak," said Salome, "we went to the tomb where Jesus was buried. When we got there we could see, even from a distance, that someone had rolled the stone away. How that happened, we don't know. The stone is so heavy. It took several strong men to roll it into place Friday evening. All we know is that now the tomb is wide open."

"We ran to the cave as fast as we could," said Mary Magdalene, who told this part of the story. "And we looked inside. Jesus' body was gone!"

"Two men in shining clothes came to us," said Joanna. " 'Why are you looking for the living among the dead?' they asked. We were scared. We didn't know what to think. No one else was around. Even the soldiers who had been guarding the tomb had gone."

"We don't know who it was who spoke to us. Maybe they were angels," Joanna continued. "They reminded us of something Jesus told us when he was alive. He said he'd

be crucified but that on the third day he would rise from the dead. This is the third day, you know, since he was crucified."

"Maybe Jesus really is alive. Maybe Jesus has risen from the dead." All the women were trying to speak at once.

"Take it easy, there," warned Thomas. "Don't start imagining things."

"We aren't imagining things. The men at the tomb said . . ."

Peter and John did not wait for the women to finish. They rushed from the room. They dashed down the outside staircase and through the narrow city streets on their way to the garden tomb. They had to see for themselves.

When they arrived at the tomb, they found it to be just as the women had said. The tomb was empty! They went in and looked for themselves. Sure enough, Jesus' body was not there. All John and Peter saw were the white linen grave cloths—nothing else. Where was Jesus' body? They did not know. They walked slowly back to the city, wondering all the while what this could all mean.

By evening Peter and John had rejoined the group of apostles and other followers in the upstairs room. The mood there was changing. There was still confusion. But, instead of fear and grief at the loss of their master, there was a growing air of excitement. Some were actually saying they had seen the Risen Christ: "As we walked on the road late this afternoon toward our home in Emmaus," said one man, "a stranger joined us. We invited him to have supper with us. As he blessed the bread and broke it, we realized that the stranger was Jesus himself."

"I have seen him, too," said Mary Magdalene. "I saw someone that I thought was the gardener near the empty tomb. I asked if he knew what had become of Jesus' body. The man I was talking to called me by name. 'Mary!' he said. And with that I recognized Jesus himself."

Other followers told similar stories. Some, however, thought those telling the tales must have lost their minds. Most did not know what to think.

Suddenly, even though the door was locked and bolted, someone stepped into their midst. The face was familiar. Most of the group trembled with fear as they blinked their eyes and realized—it was the master, Jesus.

"Don't be afraid," Jesus said. "Peace be with you."

"It's a ghost!" exclaimed John.

"No, I'm no ghost," the master laughed. "It is I, Jesus. Don't you recognize me, after all we've been through together? Look. See the scars on my wrists and feet?"

"It is the Lord!" The apostles all began to talk at once.

"Wait a minute. Let me explain everything," Jesus said, smiling at their excitement. "But first, let's prepare some of that fish I see over there so that you can eat."

Never before was there a supper like this one. Jesus explained how, from the beginning, his life and death had been part of God's plan. Now, the highpoint of the plan had come: God had raised Jesus from the dead.

One of the apostles, Thomas, was not in that room with the others that first Easter night. "The Lord has risen!" the others told Thomas when they found him. "We talked with him and ate with him last night."

"I wish that were true," Thomas said sadly. "But I'm afraid you must have been dreaming."

"His tomb is empty. You can go see for yourself."

"I heard that, but one of the guards told me that you had just stolen Jesus' body."

"Nonsense! Don't you know how that got started? Caiaphas, the high priest, bribed the guards to spread that lie."

"Well, I still have to have proof," Thomas replied. "I won't believe your story unless I see the print of the nails and put my hand in the spear wound in Jesus' side."

About a week later Jesus appeared to the apostles again in the upstairs room. This time Thomas was with them. "Thomas," said Jesus, "put your fingers in the nailprints in my wrists. Put your hand where the spear sliced into my side." Thomas did not need to do as Jesus said. He knew now that this man was Jesus. "My Lord and my God," he exclaimed.

Jesus continued to appear to the apostles. He chose different times and different places. No one knew why Jesus chose the times and places he did. But, whenever he appeared, the master always left the apostles with comforting words that would guide them in the days that lay ahead.

It seemed that one day Jesus came especially to help the Apostle Peter. Peter was the man whom Jesus had called his rock. Peter was also the apostle who had denied knowing Jesus three times the night of Jesus' trial. Peter had done this to save his own skin. He had been afraid that the guards would arrest him, too.

Peter was ashamed for what he had done. And, so far as he knew, there was no way he could make up for it.

The day before Jesus came to help Peter, all of the apostles were sitting on a beach at sundown. "I am going out on the boat to catch some fish," Peter told the others.

"Oh, we'll go with you," they all agreed.

All night long they fished from their boat. But, somehow, they could not catch a thing.

At daybreak, a stranger on the beach called out to them. "Hello out there. Have you caught any fish?"

"No," they answered, "we've caught nothing."

"Cast your net on the right side of your boat. You will find some there. Do it and see." They did as the stranger had told them. Now, for the first time, they caught fish. There were so many that they could hardly pull them in.

Peter squinted toward the shore. He had fished around this lake all his life. Who was this stranger? Then Peter

began to laugh. "It's Jesus!" Peter was so excited, he jumped into the lake and swam to shore.

When he got there, he saw that Jesus had already built a fire and cooked some fish. "Bring also some of the fish you have caught, and we will have enough breakfast for all of us," Jesus said.

After they had eaten, the master drew Peter aside. "Peter, do you love me?" Jesus asked gently.

"Yes, Lord, you know that I love you," replied Peter.

"Feed my lambs," Jesus said. Then, a second time Jesus said to Peter, "Do you love me?"

"Yes, Lord, you know that I love you."

"Then," said Jesus, "tend my sheep." A third time Jesus said, "Peter, do you love me?"

Suddenly Peter realized what this conversation was all about. Three times Peter had said he did not know Jesus, that night before Jesus died. Now, three times Jesus had asked Peter to declare his loyalty and love.

With tears in his eyes Peter said it again: "Lord, you know everything. You know that I love you."

"Feed my sheep," smiled Jesus.

Peter's heart filled with joy. He knew what Jesus meant. Jesus had forgiven him. Jesus was giving Peter work to do, too. Jesus' sheep were Jesus' people. Peter would teach the people the words of Jesus.

Some days later the Risen Christ was with his apostles again, high on a mountain. Now he called all of them to their new task: "Go into all the world and tell everyone about my words. I want people of every race and land to know that through me they can have forgiveness for their sins. And remember this: I will be with you, always!"

Jesus lifted up his hands and blessed the apostles. And then they did not see him anymore. He had returned to his Father.

Paul, missionary of Christ

The high priest looked at the young Pharisee with surprise. Who was this fiery new religious teacher? And why was the young man demanding a letter of introduction to the synagogue, the Jewish place of worship, in Damascus?

"I am Saul," the visitor explained, "Saul of Tarsus."

"Oh, I see. Yes, I've heard of you," replied the high priest, much friendlier now. "You've been helping to arrest the followers of Jesus."

"Yes. I'm very concerned about the new religion, this new Christianity. Some of the Jews have converted, have taken up this new faith. We have to get all our people back to following our traditions. Don't they realize that the real Messiah will not come until the people stop sinning?

"It's a good thing that Jesus is dead. Maybe now, we can get the people back on the right track. But, first, the Christians have to be eliminated."

"You seem determined to do that, young man."

"I was present at the execution of one of these followers of Jesus," replied Saul. "His name was Stephen. The crowd killed him with stones. It was an ugly sight, but if that's what needs to be done, so be it. That's why I'm here today with my request."

"And what is that request, my son?"

"Well, as you know, there are followers of Jesus in many places now other than Jerusalem. I would like to go to the city of Damascus and search for these people. I want authority to arrest them and to bring them back to Jerusalem for proper punishment for their crimes."

The high priest nodded. "All right. I will have an official letter prepared for you. This letter will give you the permission you need."

Saul wasted no time in starting his journey to Damascus. Beneath his robe—close to his heart—was the treasured letter from the high priest. Saul had time to think as he walked along. "I must find those Christians. They do not worship God according to tradition. What gives this new group of believers the power to cause so much trouble? Jesus of Nazareth was only a carpenter, and yet they call him the Son of God. Ridiculous!"

Suddenly, the midday sun seemed to explode. There was a glaring light all around Saul. Stunned and silent, he fell to the hot ground. "Saul!" he heard a voice say. "Saul, why do you torture me?"

"Who is talking to me?" Saul's dry lips quivered.

"I am Jesus, the one you've been fighting. Get up. Go into the city. There is work waiting for you there."

Saul turned his face toward the sky and opened his eyes. A cry escaped Saul's lips, for he saw only a sea of blackness. The young man was blind.

Fellow travelers led Saul to Damascus. There, for three days he sat, unable to see. He tried to sort out what had happened. He knew he had heard a voice on the road. He knew Jesus himself had spoken. What did it all mean?

The door to his room creaked. Saul realized he was no longer alone. Suddenly, he felt a hand on his shoulder, and he heard a gentle voice. "Brother! Brother Saul. The Lord has sent me that you might see again."

At these words Saul's sight began to return. "Who are you?" he asked the visitor.

"My name is Ananias. I am a Christian."

"Ananias," thought Saul. "Doesn't he know that I came here to arrest him and all the other Christians I could find? And, yet, he just called me 'brother.' "

Saul stood up and looked with trust into the forgiving eyes of his new friend. And Ananias baptized Saul then and there. Saul of Tarsus all at once became a new man. And, later, as he taught all over his world, people would start calling him by a new name, too. Instead of the Hebrew name Saul, the people would call him by the Greek word for the same name. They would call him Paul, the Apostle Paul.

From the moment Ananias baptized him, the Apostle Paul's life was in danger. The only safe thing to do was to hide. But, instead, the next Sabbath Paul stood up in a Damascus synagogue. "I am a convert," he announced. "I now know that Jesus is the Christ. I spoke to him as I came here to arrest Christians. Jesus is alive. Through him we will all receive forgiveness. God wants me to tell you that Jesus is the Son of God."

Saul's former friends were shocked. There was nothing to do now but try to arrest Paul. "We must have the city gates guarded day and night," they agreed. "The traitor must not escape."

Secretly, however, the Followers of the Way, as Christians were sometimes called, plotted, too. One night a group of them carried what seemed to be a basket of fish up to a house built into the wall of the city. They passed the basket through a window and slowly lowered the basket to the ground, far below. The next morning, the guards were still watching the city's gates. But Paul, who had been in the basket, was already on his way back to Jerusalem.

Meanwhile, the Christians living in Jerusalem had heard that Paul—who had once been their enemy—wanted to meet with them and worship with them. "He must be a spy," they warned one another. "Watch out for him."

But when Paul arrived, one brave Christian—Barnabas—came to Paul's side to help him. "This is my friend Paul," Barnabas said. "I know he used to be our enemy. But he is a different man now. He has met Jesus, our risen Lord. God has forgiven Paul. So must we. And God has also chosen him to do some important work. We must allow Paul to help us tell the world about Jesus."

The Christians finally accepted Paul and allowed him to join in their work. But no sooner had they done so when they learned that enemies were plotting to arrest Paul. Once again his fellow believers took action to save his life. This time they secretly whisked him away to the seacoast. There, his helpers smuggled him into a boat going to his hometown of Tarsus.

From now on, Paul's journey would never end. He became a great teacher about Jesus. He was not alone in his travels, of course. By this time, Christians were scattered all over the Roman Empire. Everywhere they went, they told the story of Jesus. This was their job, their mission.

Because they were on missions to teach about Jesus, they were called *missionaries.*

As a missionary, Paul traveled to country after country, meeting many people and teaching them about Jesus. When he arrived in a new place, he liked to go to the synagogue to worship on the Sabbath Day. Often, someone there recognized him. This is what happened in a synagogue one day when a city leader invited Paul to speak before the people gathered there.

Paul rose to his feet. "People of Israel," he said, "let me recall with you some stories about God. These are stories you have heard ever since you were boys and girls.

"Remember," Paul said to them, "how God promised Abraham that through his children all the world would be blessed? Now, through a man called Jesus, that blessing has come.

"Remember how through Moses, God rescued His people from slavery in Egypt? Now, through Jesus, God has set us free in a new way.

"Remember how God raised up the shepherd David, making him a great king? Now God has raised up another great man, Jesus—a new kind of king.

"Remember how the prophets promised that someday a Savior would come? Now the Savior Jesus has come."

And with that Paul told the listeners in the synagogue the story of how Jesus had died on the cross. He told them how God had raised Jesus from the dead on the third day. Paul explained how Jesus had sent his apostles out to tell the whole world about forgiveness and a new kind of life in Christ. "Believe in Jesus and receive his salvation!" Paul urged them.

Wherever Paul went, some did believe. Many men and women and boys and girls accepted his teaching. But many did not know what to think. And some tried to keep Paul from preaching about Jesus. He was always in danger.

In the city of Lystra, for example, his enemies threw rocks and stones at him until they thought he was dead. They dragged his bruised and bleeding body outside the city wall and left it there. The believers had watched helplessly as they saw stone after stone thrown at Paul. Now they gathered around his body to mourn and grieve.

"He was a hero for Christ, but now he is dead," sobbed the believers.

As the group stood around, someone suddenly broke the silence: "Look, I think I saw an eyelid move."

"I think you're right." The person who had spoken leaned over and put his ear on Paul's chest. "There's a faint heartbeat. We must hurry to bandage his wounds. He is still alive."

Praising God, they took Paul to a home in the city. There, the believers washed his wounds. The risk of death did not stop Paul from teaching about Jesus. The following day, he was on his way to yet another town.

In the city of Philippi, the police arrested Paul and his friend Silas, another missionary, for trying to spread the new faith. The police stripped the coats from Paul's and Silas' backs. "Whip them!" shouted the city official in charge. "We must teach them a lesson. Beat them with heavy rods and then lock them in jail."

The police did as they were told. Then the jailer put Paul and Silas into a cell that was in the darkest part of the prison. He also bound them in chains. "That should hold you two. You'll not escape from my prison," the jailer said as he left them alone.

The hours ticked by. Paul and Silas could feel the blood running down their backs from their beating that morning. Yet, their pain did not stop them from praying. They even sang joyful songs of praise to God.

Suddenly, about midnight, there was a great earthquake. The prison shook to its base. All the doors swung open.

The chains fell from the prisoners' hands and feet. The jailer woke up. When he saw that the prison doors were all open, he thought that all his prisoners had escaped.

"Don't worry," laughed Paul, "the prisoners are here."

But the jailer was still terrified. "Bring me a lantern," he called to his wife. "If my prisoners have escaped, for my carelessness the Romans will kill me in the morning. What will I do? What must I do to be saved?"

Paul knew what the jailer really needed. "Believe in the Lord Jesus Christ and you will be saved—you and your wife and your boys and girls, too," Paul told him. Something in Paul's voice gave the frightened jailer courage. He wanted to hear more.

Finding that the prisoners really were still there after all, he took Paul and Silas to his own room, bandaged their wounds, and listened as they told him about Jesus. Before morning, Paul and Silas had baptized the jailer and all his family as Christians, too.

The years went by as Paul continued his missionary work. He helped people of every race become a part of the Christian church. But Paul faced more and more danger.

Near the end of his life, he returned to Jerusalem. There, a riot broke out against him. Many people did not want him interfering with the temple in Jerusalem and with the way they worshipped God.

"Kill him!" shouted the mob. Only the quick arrival of Roman soldiers saved Paul's life. They carried him in chains to their fort.

By the next day, the leaders of the mob had another plan to get rid of Paul. They went to the chief priests and said, "Send for Paul to come and speak to you. Forty of us will wait in ambush and kill him before he ever gets here."

But Paul found out about the plot. He sent word of it to the Roman commander, who listened carefully. "Don't worry," the commander told the messenger, "I am going to put an end to this trouble before the rioting gets worse. We must maintain law and order in Jerusalem.

"Get two hundred soldiers ready and seventy horsemen and two hundred spearmen," he commanded to his men. "Be ready to leave after nightfall. Get a horse ready for Paul to ride, too. We must get him out of Jerusalem."

Paul would have to stand trial. His crime was heresy, a serious crime in those times. *Heresy* meant holding a belief different from the accepted belief of your group. In Paul's case, he was helping spread Christianity in an area where there were other religions with many, many followers. Some people resented Paul's attempts to bring new believers over to the side of Christianity. They felt he was a dangerous troublemaker.

To receive a fair trial, Paul finally appealed his case to the supreme court in Rome, far away from Jerusalem and his enemies there. In chains, Paul came at last to the capital of the Roman Empire. It had been his dream to teach about Jesus here. And now he would teach in Rome, even if he had to do so in chains.

As Paul awaited his trial, he thought about all that had happened to him during his lifetime. He remembered how he had started out by hunting down Christians to punish them for their faith. And he remembered hearing Jesus on the Damascus road and becoming a Christian, himself. Many times he had been stoned and beaten, and he had been put in chains in rat-infested prisons. He also recalled when he and Silas had sung songs in praise of God from a prison cell. The Apostle Paul had been hungry and thirsty and cold many times.

As he sat here in chains and thought about his life, one thing was sure. He was a prisoner, but the faith was free. Other missionaries carried out Paul's work, even as he remained locked in his dreary cell. And they would continue to carry out his work to this day.

Best-loved inspirational songs

Jesus loves me

Jesus loves me, this I know,
For the Bible tells me so;
Little ones to him belong;
They are weak, but he is strong.
  Yes, Jesus loves me,
  Yes, Jesus loves me,
  Yes, Jesus loves me
  The Bible tells me so.

Silent night

Silent night, holy night!
All is calm, all is bright;
Round yon virgin mother and child,
Holy infant so tender and mild:
Sleep in heavenly peace,
Sleep in heavenly peace.

Silent night, holy night!
Darkness flies, all is light;
Shepherds hear the angels sing:
Alleluia! Hail the king!
Christ the Savior is born,
Christ the Savior is born.

Rock of ages

Rock of ages, cleft for me,
Let me hide myself in thee;
Let the water and the blood,
From thy side, a healing flood,
Be of sin the double cure,
Save from wrath, and make me pure.

Should my tears forever flow,
Should my zeal no languor know,
All for sin could not atone,
Thou must save, and thou alone;
In my hand no price I bring,
Simply to thy cross I cling.

Go, tell it on the mountains

When I was a learner, I sought both night and day,
I asked the Lord to aid me, and He showed me the way.
Go, tell it on the mountains,
Over the hills an' everywhere,
Go, tell it on the mountains,
Our Jesus Christ is born.
Go over the hills an' everywhere,
Go, tell it on the mountains, go!

He made me a watchman upon the city wall
An' if I am a Christian I am the least of all.
Go, tell it on the mountains,
Over the hills an' everywhere,
Go, tell it on the mountains,
Our Jesus Christ is born.

Lo, how a rose e'er blooming

Lo, how a rose e'er blooming
From tender stem hath sprung,
Of Jesse's lineage coming
As men of old have sung.
It came, a floweret bright,
Amid the cold of winter
When half spent was the night.

Isaiah 'twas foretold it,
The rose I have in mind,
With Mary we behold it,
The virgin mother kind.
To show God's love aright
She bore to men a Savior,
When half spent was the night.

Fairest Lord Jesus

Fairest Lord Jesus,
Ruler of all nature,
O, thou of God and man the Son,
Thee will I cherish,
Thee will I honor,
Thou, my soul's glory, joy and crown.

Fair are the meadows,
Fairer still the woodlands
Robed in the blooming garb of spring;
Jesus is fairer,
Jesus is purer,
Who makes the woeful heart to sing.

Onward, Christian soldiers

Onward, Christian soldiers,
Marching as to war,
With the cross of Jesus
Going on before.
Christ, the royal master,
Leads against the foe;
Forward into battle,
See, his banners go.
Onward, Christian soldiers,
Marching as to war,
With the cross of Jesus
Going on before.

What child is this?

What child is this, who, laid to rest,
On Mary's lap is sleeping?
Whom angels greet with anthems sweet,
While shepherds watch are keeping?
This, this is Christ the King;
Whom shepherds guard and angels sing:
Haste, haste to bring him laud,
The babe, the Son of Mary.

Why lies he in such mean estate,
Where ox and ass are feeding?
Good Christian, fear, for sinners here
The silent word is pleading;
Nails, spear, shall pierce him through,
The cross be borne for me, for you:
Hail, hail, the Word made flesh,
The babe, the Son of Mary.

Bring a torch, Jeannette, Isabella!

Bring a torch, Jeannette, Isabella.
Bring a torch, to the cradle run!
It is Jesus, good folk of the village,
Christ is born and Mary's calling.
Ah, ah, beautiful is the mother;
Ah, ah, beautiful is her son.

It is wrong when the child is sleeping,
It is wrong to talk so loud;
Silence, all, as you gather around,
Lest your noise should waken Jesus:
Hush, hush, see how fast he slumbers;
Hush, hush, see how fast he sleeps.

Were you there when they crucified my Lord?

Were you there when they crucified my Lord?
Were you there when they crucified my Lord?
Oh, sometimes it causes me to tremble, tremble, tremble.
Were you there when they crucified my Lord?

Were you there when they nailed him to a tree?
Were you there when they nailed him to a tree?
Oh, sometimes it causes me to tremble, tremble, tremble.
Were you there when they nailed him to a tree?

Were you there when they laid him in the tomb?
Were you there when they laid him in the tomb?
Oh, sometimes it causes me to tremble, tremble, tremble.
Were you there when they laid him in the tomb?

Come, ye thankful people, come

Come, ye thankful people, come,
Raise the song of harvest home:
All is safely gathered in,
Ere the winter storms begin;
God, our Maker, doth provide
For our wants to be supplied:
Come to God's own temple, come,
Raise the song of harvest home.

All the world is God's own field,
Fruit unto His praise to yield;
Wheat and tares together sown,
Unto joy or sorrow grown
First the blade, and then the ear,
Then the full corn shall appear:
Lord of harvest, grant that we
Wholesome grain and pure may be.

Oh, holy night

Oh, holy night, the stars are brightly shining,
It is the night of the dear Savior's birth.
Long lay the world in sin and error pining,
Till he appeared and the soul felt its worth.
A thrill of hope, the weary world rejoices,
For yonder breaks a new and glorious morn.
  Fall on your knees.
  Oh, hear the angel voices!
  Oh, night divine;
  Oh, night when Christ was born.
  Oh, night divine!
  Oh, night. Oh, night divine!

God of our Fathers, Whose almighty hand

God of our Fathers, Whose almighty hand
Leads forth in beauty all the starry band
Of shining worlds in splendor through the skies,
Our grateful songs before Thy throne arise.

Thy love divine hath led us in the past;
In this free land by Thee our lot is cast;
Be Thou our ruler, guardian, guide, and stay;
Thy word our law,
Thy paths our chosen way.

A mighty fortress is our God

A mighty fortress is our God,
A bulwark never failing;
Our helper He, amid the flood
Of mortal ills prevailing.
For still our ancient foe
Doth seek to work us woe;
His craft and pow'r are great,
And arm'd with cruel hate,
On earth is not his equal.

Did we in our own strength confide,
Our striving would be losing;
Were not the right man on our side,
The man of God's own choosing.
Dost ask who that may be?
Christ Jesus, it is he;
Lord Sabaoth his name,
From age to age the same,
And he must win the battle.

Away in a manger

Away in a manger,
No crib for a bed
The little Lord Jesus
Laid down his sweet head;
The stars in the sky
Looked down where he lay,
The little Lord Jesus
Asleep on the hay.

The cattle are lowing,
The poor baby wakes,
But little Lord Jesus
No crying he makes;
I love thee, Lord Jesus.
Look down from the sky,
And stay by my cradle
Till morning is nigh.

Oh, come, oh, come, Emmanuel

Oh come, oh come, Emmanuel,
And ransom captive Israel,
That mourns in lonely exile here
Until the Son of God appear.
  Refrain:
  Rejoice! Rejoice! Emmanuel
  Shall come to thee, oh Israel.

Oh come, thou rod of Jesse's stem,
From every foe deliver them
That trust thy mighty power to save,
And give them victory o'er the grave. *(Refrain.)*

Swing low, sweet chariot

Refrain:
Swing low, sweet chariot
Coming for to carry me home
Swing low, sweet chariot
Coming for to carry me home.

I looked over Jordan and what did I see,
Coming for to carry me home?
A band of angels coming after me,
Coming for to carry me home. *(Refrain.)*

If you get there before I do,
Coming for to carry me home,
Tell all my friends I'm coming too,
Coming for to carry me home. *(Refrain.)*

I'm sometimes up and sometimes down,
Coming for to carry me home,
But still my soul feels heavenly bound
Coming for to carry me home. *(Refrain.)*

Abide with me

Abide with me:
Fast falls the eventide;
The darkness deepens;
Lord, with me abide!
When other helpers fail,
And comforts flee,
Help of the helpless, oh abide with me.

Oh come, all ye faithful

Oh come, all ye faithful,
Joyful and triumphant,
Oh come ye, oh come ye to Bethlehem.
Come and behold him,
Born the king of angels.
  Refrain:
  Oh come, let us adore him,
  Oh come, let us adore him,
  Oh come, let us adore him,
  Christ, the Lord!

Oh sing, choirs of angels,
Sing in exultation,
Oh sing, all ye citizens of heaven above.
Glory to God,
All glory in the highest! *(Refrain.)*

Yea, Lord, we greet thee,
Born this happy morning,
Oh Jesus, to thee be all glory given;
Word of the Father,
Now in flesh appearing! *(Refrain.)*

Favorite quotes from the New Testament

In the days of Herod the king, behold, there came wise men from the east to Jerusalem, saying, Where is he that is born King of the Jews? for we have seen his star in the east, and are come to worship him.

Matthew 2:1–2

The voice of one crying in the wilderness, Prepare ye the way of the Lord, make His paths straight.

Matthew 3:3

Thou shalt not tempt the Lord thy God.

Matthew 4:7

Blessed are the poor in spirit: for theirs is the Kingdom of Heaven. Blessed are they that mourn: for they shall be comforted. Blessed are the meek: for they shall inherit the earth. Blessed are they which do hunger and thirst after righteousness: for they shall be filled. Blessed are the merciful: for they shall obtain mercy. Blessed are the pure in heart: for they shall see God. Blessed are the peacemakers: for they shall be called the children of God.

Matthew 5:3–9

Swear not at all; neither by heaven; for it is God's throne: Nor by the earth, for it is His footstool: neither by Jerusalem; for it is the city of the great King. Neither shalt thou swear by thy head, because thou canst not make one hair white or black.

Matthew 5:34–36

Resist not evil: but whosoever shall smite thee on thy right cheek, turn to him the other also.

Matthew 5:39

Lay not up for yourselves treasures upon earth, where moth and rust doth corrupt, and where thieves break through and steal. Lay up for yourselves treasures in heaven.

Matthew 6:19–20

No man can serve two masters. Ye cannot serve God and mammon.

Matthew 6:24

Consider the lilies of the field, how they grow; they toil not, neither do they spin: And yet I say unto you, that even Solomon in all his glory was not arrayed like one of these.

Matthew 6:28–29

Judge not, that ye be not judged.

Matthew 7:1

Ask, and it shall be given you; seek, and ye shall find; knock, and it shall be opened unto you.

Matthew 7:8

Or what man is there of you, whom if his son ask bread, will he give him a stone?

Matthew 7:9

Wide is the gate, and broad is the way, that leadeth to destruction, and many there be that go in thereat. Strait is the gate, and narrow is the way, which leadeth unto life, and few there be that find it.

Matthew 7:13–14

Let the dead bury their dead.

Matthew 8:22

Come unto me, all ye that labour and are heavy laden, and I will give you rest. Take my yoke upon you, and learn of me; for I am meek and lowly in heart: and ye shall find rest unto your souls. For my yoke is easy, and my burden is light.

Matthew 11:28–30

He that is not with me is against me; and he that gathereth not with me scattereth abroad.

Matthew 12:30
Luke 11:23

They be blind leaders of the blind. And if the blind lead the blind, both shall fall into the ditch.

Matthew 15:14

Thou art Peter, and upon this rock I will build my church; and the gates of hell shall not prevail against it. And I will give unto thee the keys to the Kingdom of Heaven.

Matthew 16:18–19

Get thee behind me, Satan.

Matthew 16:23

And if thine eye offend thee, pluck it out, and cast it from thee; it is better for thee to enter into life with one eye, rather than having two eyes to be cast into hell fire.

Matthew 18:9

For where two or three are gathered together in my name, there am I in the midst of them.

Matthew 18:20

What therefore God hath joined together, let not man put asunder.

Matthew 19:6

Thou shalt love thy neighbour as thyself.

Matthew 19:19

If thou wilt be perfect, go and sell that thou hast, and give it to the poor, and thou shalt have treasure in heaven: and come and follow me.

Matthew 19:21

A rich man shall hardly enter into the Kingdom of Heaven. It is easier for a camel to go through the eye of a needle, than for a rich man to enter into the Kingdom of God.

Matthew 19:23–24

With men this is impossible; but with God all things are possible.

Matthew 19:26

It is written, My house shall be called the house of prayer; but ye have made it a den of thieves.

Matthew 21:13

Render therefore unto Caesar the things which are Caesar's.

Matthew 22:21

This night, before the cock crow, thou shalt deny me thrice.

Matthew 26:34

If it be possible, let this cup pass from me.

Matthew 26:39

The spirit indeed is willing, but the flesh is weak.

Matthew 26:41

All they that take the sword shall perish with the sword.

Matthew 26:52

He [Pilate] took water, and washed his hands before the multitude, saying, I am innocent of the blood of this just person.

Matthew 27:24

My God, my God, why hast Thou forsaken me?

Matthew 27:46

For what shall it profit a man, if he shall gain the whole world, and lose his own soul? Or what shall a man give in exchange for his soul?

Mark 8:36–37

Suffer the little children to come unto me, and forbid them not: for of such is the Kingdom of God.

Mark 10:14

Hail, thou that art highly favoured, the Lord is with thee: blessed art thou among women.

Luke 1:28

My soul doth magnify the Lord, and my spirit hath rejoiced in God my Saviour. For He hath regarded the low estate of His handmaiden: for, behold, from henceforth all generations shall call me blessed.

Luke 1:46–48

To give light to them that sit in darkness and in the shadow of death, to guide our feet into the way of peace.

Luke 1:79

And it came to pass in those days, that there went out a decree from Caesar Augustus, that all the world should be taxed.

Luke 2:1

And, lo, the angel of the Lord came upon them, and the glory of the Lord shone round about them: and they were sore afraid.

Luke 2:9

Glory to God in the highest, and on earth peace, good will toward men.

Luke 2:14

Lord, now lettest Thou Thy servant depart in peace, according to Thy word.

Luke 2:29

Physician, heal thyself.

Luke 4:23

Joy shall be in heaven over one sinner that repenteth.

Luke 15:7

The Kingdom of God is within you.

Luke 17:21

God be merciful to me a sinner.

Luke 18:13

For if they do these things in a green tree, what shall be done in the dry?

Luke 23:31

Father, forgive them; for they know not what they do.

Luke 23:34

Father, into Thy hands I commend my spirit.

Luke 23:46

God so loved the world, that He gave His only begotten Son, that whosoever believeth in him should not perish, but have everlasting life. For God sent not his Son into the world to condemn the world; but that the world through him might be saved.

John 3:16–17

He that is without sin among you, let him first cast a stone at her. . . . And they that heard it, being convicted by their own conscience, went one by one.

John 8:7, 9

I am the resurrection, and the life: he that believeth in me though he were dead, yet shall he live: and whosoever liveth and believeth in me shall never die.

John 11:25

I am the way, the truth, and the life: no man cometh unto the Father, but by me.

John 14:6

Greater love hath no man than this, that a man lay down his life for his friends.

John 15:13

Woman, behold thy son! . . . Behold thy mother!

John 19:26–27

Blessed are they that have not seen, and yet have believed.

John 20:29

It is more blessed to give than to receive.

Acts 20:35

Christ being raised from the dead dieth no more.

Romans 6:9

If God be for us, who can be against us?

Romans 8:31

Though I have all faith, so that I could remove mountains, and have not charity, I am nothing. And though I bestow all my goods to feed the poor, and though I give my body to be burned, and have not charity, it profiteth me nothing. Charity suffereth long, and is kind; charity envieth not; charity vaunteth not itself, is not puffed up, doth not behave itself unseemly, seeketh not her own, is not easily provoked, thinketh no evil; rejoiceth not in iniquity, but rejoiceth in the truth; beareth all things, believeth all things, hopeth all things, endureth all things. Charity never faileth.

1 Corinthians 13:2–8

And now abideth faith, hope, and charity, these three; but the greatest of these is charity.

1 Corinthians 13:13

Whatsoever a man soweth, that shall he also reap.

Galatians 6:7

Be ye angry, and sin not: let not the sun go down upon your wrath.

Ephesians 4:26

The love of money is the root of all evil.

1 Timothy 6:10

I have fought a good fight, I have finished my course, I have kept the faith.

2 Timothy 4:7

Let brotherly love continue. Be not forgetful to entertain strangers: for thereby some have entertained angels unawares.

Hebrews 13:1

He that loveth not knoweth not God; for God is love.

1 John 4:8

I am Alpha and Omega, the beginning and the ending, saith the Lord.

Revelation 1:8

Glossary

On the following pages, you will find material that will help you to understand and use all the sections of *Best-loved Bible Stories,* as well as the Bible itself. The first section lists many terms that appear in the Bible or are used in connection with Biblical topics or events. Included are the names of persons and places important to understanding Bible material.

The second section lists the titles of all the Old and New Testament stories upon which the events described in *Best-loved Bible Stories* have been based. Next to each story title, the story's episode or episodes are briefly noted. Each episode description concludes with a notation of the book, chapter, and—when needed—verses where the episode appears in the Bible.

When you look up a term or name in the first section, you may be surprised at some of the definitions and explanations. Here's an example: the word *cross.* It can mean "angry," and it can also mean "to go across." Yet, we have defined *cross* only as an "execution device" and a "symbol of the Christian religion." Our definitions and explanations are limited: they cover only the way the words and names are used in a Biblical or spiritual sense.

The second section, "Biblical sources," may look complicated to use, but it is not. Take the story "Noah and the ark." Its title appears in dark letters. Then comes the episode: God saves Noah and his family from the flood. Next, in parentheses, comes the episode's location in the Bible: Gen. 6–9:17. *Gen.* stands for Genesis, the first book in the Bible; 6–9 are the chapters of Genesis that cover the story of Noah; and 17 is the verse of chapter 9 where the episode ends. Remember that whenever you see a colon (:), the number that follows is a verse number, not a chapter number. Also, if you are not sure which book of the Bible an abbreviation stands for, you may look the abbreviation up on page 31 of the Old Testament volume.

Biblical terms and names

abide to stay with; live
adore to worship; love
adversity unhappiness; misfortune; distress
Alexandria an Egyptian city on the Mediterranean Sea; in the time of Jesus, a major port city for the Roman Empire
alleluia, also **hallelujah** "praise ye the Lord"
almighty having great power
alpha and omega the first and last

letters of the Greek alphabet; the equivalent of "from *a* to *z*"
altar a table or stand, usually in the most sacred part of a church, synagogue, or temple, always thought of as the central point of worship
amen Hebrew for "so be it" and "may it come true"; *amen* is said after a prayer, a wish, or a statement with which one agrees
Ananias an early Christian sent to the Apostle Paul at his conversion and who was a means of restoring Paul's sight
ancestor a person from whom one is directly descended, usually more remote than a parent, such as a grandparent, great-grandparent, and so on
angel a messenger of God; in some religions, one of an order of spiritual beings that are attendants of God
anoint to apply oil
anthem a song of praise
apostle one of the twelve disciples chosen by Jesus to go forth and preach the gospel to all the world
ark the large boat in which Noah saved himself, his family, and a pair of each kind of animal from the flood
Ark of the Covenant the wooden chest or box in which the Israelites kept the two stone tablets containing the Ten Commandments
arrayed dressed
ascend to go up; rise; move upward
ascension the passing of Christ from earth to heaven
Asia Minor a peninsula of western Asia between the Black Sea and the Mediterranean Sea; today, a region occupied mainly by Turkey
Assyria north of Babylonia in Mesopotamia, an ancient country known for its military triumphs and great warriors
astrologer a person who claims to know and interpret the supposed influence of the stars and planets on persons and events
asunder in pieces
Athens a famed Greek city of culture and learning, the ancient center of science, literature, and art
atone to make amends, make up
avenger a person who gets revenge for a wrong

Babylon one of the great cities of the ancient world; a trading center and the capital and religious center of the ancient kingdom of Babylonia, south of Assyria in Mesopotamia
baptism the act of dipping a person into water, or sprinkling water on the person, as a sign of washing away sin and of admission into the Christian church
barley the seed or grain of a cereal grass usually used to feed livestock; in small villages, a grain whose flour is sometimes baked into round, flat loaves of bread
Barnabas a great friend and helper of the Apostle Paul in his missionary work
barren unable to have children
Beatitudes the eight verses in the Sermon on the Mount that begin with the word *blessed*
begotten given birth to or having become a father
bestow to give
Bethany a suburb of Jerusalem where Jesus often stayed in the home of his friends Lazarus, Martha, and Mary
Bethel a town about 12 miles north of Jerusalem, associated with many episodes in the Bible, including the story of Jacob's ladder and the reign of Jeroboam
Bethlehem an ancient town in Galilee, south of Jerusalem; the birthplace of Jesus
birthright the rights belonging to persons because they are the oldest, because they were born in a

certain country, or because of any other fact of their birth
blasphemy lack of respect for God or sacred objects
blessing a prayer asking God to show His favor; a giving of God's favor
bulrush a tall, slender plant that grows in wet places like riverbanks, used in weaving baskets, mats, and the like; papyrus
bulwark a defense or protection
burning bush the flaming bush on Mount Sinai from which God spoke to Moses
burnt offering a sacrifice placed on an altar and burned completely as a gift to a god, goddess, or idol

Caesar the title of the Roman emperors from 27 BC to AD 138
Calvary the place outside ancient Jerusalem where Jesus died on the cross; also called Golgotha
Cana an ancient city in northern Palestine, identified as the scene of Jesus' first miracle
Canaan a region in Palestine between the Jordan River and the Mediterranean Sea; God is said to have promised Canaan to Abraham and his descendants, the Hebrews
caravan a group of merchants, pilgrims, or the like, traveling together for safety through difficult or dangerous country
carol a hymn of joy, especially at Christmas
cast to throw
cedars of Lebanon trees growing in Lebanon, at the eastern end of the Mediterranean Sea; wood used in the construction of Solomon's temple in Jerusalem
centurion in the ancient Roman army, a commander of about 100 soldiers
chaff stiff, strawlike bits around the grains of wheat, oats, and rye, separated from the grain by thrashing, or tossing, the grain about violently in a container
chariot a two-wheeled carriage pulled by horses, used in ancient times for fighting, racing, and processions
charity generous giving; kindness; love of fellow human beings
charosheth for the Passover feast, a paste made of apples, raisins, nuts, and cinnamon; a symbol of the suffering of the ancient Hebrews when they were slaves to the Egyptians
cherub plural **cherubim,** an angel in the second highest order of angels, just below the **seraphim**
Christian a person who believes in Jesus and follows his teachings; a person belonging to the religion of Jesus
Christianity the religion taught by Jesus and his followers; Christian beliefs or faiths
church a building for public Christian worship or religious services
Church, the all Christians
circumcision in the Jewish ritual, a boy is circumcised when he is 8 days old as a symbol of God's covenant, or agreement, with Abraham
clan a group of related families that claim to be descended from the same ancestor
cloak a long, loose outer garment worn by women and men
coat of many colors a beautiful coat Jacob gave to his son Joseph, later soaked in blood by Joseph's half brothers to convince Jacob that Joseph had died of wounds
comeliness the condition of being pleasant to look at; handsomeness
commandment any rule, law, order, or direction
conceive to become pregnant
congregation a group of persons gathered together for religious worship or instruction
convert to change from one religious

belief to another or from a lack of belief to faith

Corinth an important city in ancient Greece where the Apostle Paul founded a church after his visit there in AD 51

corrupt to make evil or wicked

council a group of persons called together to give advice and to discuss or settle questions

counsel a person or group of persons that gives advice, sometimes about the law

countenance face

covenant a solemn promise; an agreement between God and humankind

creation the act of making a thing that has not been made before, as God creating the universe

cross the execution device made of a vertical pole and a crossbar, upon which Jesus was hanged; a symbol of the Christian religion

crown of thorns interwoven, thorny branches that the Roman soldiers placed on Jesus' head just before his crucifixion as a sign of mockery

crucifixion a method of execution by hanging on a cross

cubit an ancient measure of length, about 18–22 inches

curse to ask God to bring evil or harm on someone or something

cypress a cone-bearing evergreen tree that has small, scalelike leaves and light brown wood

Cyrus, King of Persia in 538 BC, the Persian ruler who decreed that the Jews residing in Babylon could return to Jerusalem and rebuild the city and its temple

Damascus founded about 3000 BC, one of the older cities of the world, important during the Assyrian and Roman Empires, among others

Day of Judgment the day of God's final judgment of humankind; the end of the world

Dead Sea a body of salt water located at the mouth of the Jordan River; in the time of Jesus, its shores were a refuge for those wishing to escape the city to live in the wilderness

deceitfully in a false, lying way

decree an official order

demon an evil spirit; devil; fiend

descendant a person born of a certain family or group; offspring, as a child, great-grandchild, and so on

devil any evil spirit; fiend; demon

disciple a follower, as a follower of Jesus, especially one of the twelve apostles

divine given by or coming from God

dominion rule; control

dwell to live

Easter the yearly celebration of the day on which Jesus is said to have risen from the grave

Eden the garden where Adam and Eve first lived; Paradise

edict a public order, decree

Egypt a nation in the northeastern corner of Africa; in ancient times, the land of the pharaohs and the location of the great pyramids

elder one of the older and more influential men of a tribe or community

embrace to hold in one's arms fondly

envy dislike for someone who has what one wants

Euphrates River a great, long river, far to the east of Palestine; in the time of King David, the Hebrew kingdom is said to have extended to the Euphrates River

eventide evening

exile to make leave home or country, often by law as a punishment; to banish

exodus a departure, usually of a large number of people, as in the exodus of Moses and the Israelites from Egypt

exultation great rejoicing
Ezra the scribe a Jewish priest regarded as having much to do with the arrangement of the earlier books of the Bible; a devout and greatly influential man

faith believing without proof
famine a lack of food in a place; a time of starvation
fast to go without food
Father in the Bible, a title of respect used for God
father of nations a title used for Abraham, Israel's ancestor
fathers of Israel a title used for the ancestors of the people of Israel, such as Abraham, Isaac, and Jacob
fathom a unit of measure equal to 6 feet (1.83 meters)
favour special treatment
Felix a cruel ruler appointed as Judea's Roman procurator in AD 53: it was Felix who brought the Apostle Paul to trial in Caesarea, keeping him in prison two years in the hope of forcing money from him
Festus Roman procurator of Judea from whom Paul appealed to Caesar and was sent to Rome for trial
flask any bottle-shaped container
flock a group of animals of one kind kept, fed, and herded together, especially sheep; people of the same group, as the early Christians were Jesus' flock
flood, the the waters that covered the earth in the time of Noah
Followers of the Way a name sometimes used for Christians
forefather an ancestor
forerunner a person who goes before or is sent ahead to show that another person is coming
forsake to abandon
founder a person who sets up something
frankincense a tree sap that gives off a sweet, spicy odor when burned
free will the ability to do something of one's own accord, or voluntarily
fruitful having good results; producing an abundance of anything

Galilee the northernmost division of Palestine in the time of Jesus, the area where he carried out much of his teaching
Garden of Gethsemane a garden near Jerusalem, the place where Judas betrayed Jesus with a kiss
generation all the people born in the same period of time; one step in the descent of a family
gentile a person who is not a Jew, especially a Christian
glean to gather grain or other crops left over in already harvested fields
goblet a drinking glass that stands high above its base on a stem, and has no handle
god, goddess a being thought to have greater powers than any human and so considered worthy of worship
God of our Fathers a title of respect for the Lord, signifying that He is the God of the ancestors of the Israelites
God's Law the Ten Commandments and other rules said to be the commandments of God
golden bull, golden calf statues worshipped as gods, in ancient times by the Canaanites and many Israelites, among others
Gomorrah an ancient, wicked city near the Dead Sea, said to have been destroyed along with the city of Sodom when God sent fire from heaven
gospel the teaching of Jesus and the apostles
governor of the feast for ancient Jewish weddings, the overseer who tested the wine and made sure the servants kept the tables full of food
gracious pleasant; kind; merciful

graven image a statue; an idol; a false god or goddess

hallelujah also **alleluia,** "praise ye the Lord"
Hamitic having to do with the Hamites, groups of people in northern and Eastern Africa said to have descended from Noah's son Ham
handmaiden servant
Haran Abraham's brother and Lot's father; also a city in Mesopotamia where many of Abraham's relatives lived
haughty proud
heaven in Christianity and some other religions, the place where God and the angels live and where the blessed go after death
Hebrew a person belonging to the Semitic tribe or nation descended from Abraham, Isaac, and Jacob; an Israelite or Jew
heir a person who has the right to a person's property or title after that person's death
hell in Christianity and some other religions, the place where wicked persons are punished after death; where the devil and condemned spirits dwell
herb a plant whose leaves or stems are used for medicine, seasoning, food, or perfume
herder one who takes care of a herd, especially of cattle or goats
heresy a belief different from the accepted belief of a given community or other kind of group
heretic a person who holds a belief different from the accepted belief of a given community or other kind of group
Herod the name of several rulers over ancient Palestine
high priest a chief priest; the head of the ancient Jewish priesthood
Holy Ghost the spirit of God; Holy Spirit
Holy of Holies the inner shrine in the Jewish temple; a most sacred shrine
Holy Scriptures the Bible
Holy Spirit Holy Ghost
hosanna a shout of praise to God; hallelujah
host a large number
hymn a song in praise of God
hypocrite a person who pretends to be what she or he is not; especially one who pretends to be good or religious

idol an image or other object that is worshipped as a god; a false god
image a likeness made of stone, wood, or some other material; a statue
incense a substance giving off a sweet smell when burned, such as frankincense; the perfume or smoke of the burning substance
inherit to receive or have as one's own after someone dies; to receive as an heir
inheritance property or title received by an heir upon the death of its owner
iniquity sin
inspirational showing God's influence on the mind or soul of humankind
Israel another name of Jacob; a name given to Abraham, Isaac, and Jacob's descendants; a people or group regarded as chosen by God; the Hebrew nation

Jabbok a stream east of the Jordan River, the site of the struggle between Jacob and the angel
Jacob's ladder Jacob's vision of a golden ladder filled with angels, reaching from Bethel into heaven; the vision through which Jacob received God's protection
Jericho a city in Jordan, north of the Dead Sea, destroyed by Joshua
Jerusalem a holy city of the Jews

and Christians, the ancient capital of the united Israelite tribes and later of Judah; location of capture, trial, and execution of Jesus

Jesse the father of King David

Jew a person descended from the Semitic people led by Moses, who settled Palestine, living there from about 1200 BC to AD 70, and who since have lived in many countries, including modern Israel; a Hebrew; an Israelite

Joppa a seaport city northwest of Jerusalem where Jonah boarded a ship in order to be able to sail away and escape doing God's bidding

Jordan River also River Jordan, the only important river of Israel and Jordan, flowing for about 100 miles; an important river in the Bible, where episodes concerning Joshua, Elijah, Jesus, and John the Baptist take place, among others

Judah an ancient Hebrew kingdom in southern Palestine made up of the tribes of Judah and Benjamin, with Jerusalem as its capital; later called Judea under the Romans

Judea the Roman name for the country in the southern part of Palestine, originally called Judah

Judges military leaders of the Hebrew tribes when they lacked a central government after King David

kin, kinspeople a person's family or relatives

labour work

laden burdened

lamb a young sheep

Lamb of God Jesus; the Messiah

Land of Nod the country to which Cain traveled after slaying his brother Abel

langour weakness, lack of energy

Last Supper the supper shared among Jesus and his apostles in Jerusalem the night before his crucifixion

laud to praise highly

leaven any material, such as yeast, that will cause dough to rise

Lebanon a great Phoenician trading empire from which Solomon obtained the cedar wood for the Temple of Jerusalem

lentil a food plant belonging to the pea family and having small, flat seeds

Levite a member of the tribe of Levi, from which assistants to the Jewish priests were traditionally chosen

lice flat-bodied, small, wingless insects that infest people's skin and hair, sucking blood and causing great irritation

lineage a family or race; ancestry

locust a kind of grasshopper that sometimes comes in great swarms, destroying crops

Lord of Hosts God

Lord's Prayer also *pater noster* (Latin for the first two words of the prayer, *Our Father*), the most widely said Christian prayer, by tradition one of the three basic statements of Christian faith; the prayer appears in two forms in the New Testament

lowing mooing

magnify to praise highly

mammon riches thought of as evil; material wealth

mandrake an herb whose root, when eaten, once was said to aid a woman to become pregnant

manger a box or trough in a barn or stable, built against the wall at the right height for horses and cattle to eat from

manna the breadlike food from heaven that God sent the Israelites as they wandered in the wilderness

mark of Cain a strange mark God placed on Cain's forehead to single him out as one not to be harmed

martyr a person who is put to death or made to suffer greatly because of his or her religious beliefs

Mede a person who was born or lived in Media, an ancient country in southwestern Asia

meditate to think quietly, seriously, and deeply

Mediterranean Sea one of the world's chief trade routes since ancient times; an area where many early civilizations, including those of Egypt, Phoenicia, and Rome, developed; the area through which early Christianity first spread

merchant a person who buys and sells for profit; a trader

Mesopotamia an ancient country in southwestern Asia between the Tigris and Euphrates rivers

messiah a savior, liberator or deliverer; when capped, as **Messiah,** the leader and liberator of the Jews—in some religions, Jesus

Midianite a member of a wandering northwestern Arabian tribe that fought against the Israelites, particularly the Judge Gideon

migrate to move from one place to another

ministry time of service as a religious guide or leader

miracle a wonderful happening that is beyond known laws of nature

missionary a person sent out to work for a religious cause or belief, often to distant areas of the world

Moab an ancient kingdom to the east and south of the Israelites; Ruth's homeland

mockery a making fun of; derision

money changer a person whose business it is to exchange money at a fixed or authorized rate, usually money of one country for that of another

Moriah the land where God commanded Abraham to go in order to sacrifice his son Isaac

mortal sure to die sometime; all living creatures

mount a mountain or a high hill

Mount Carmel in Palestine, a 13-mile long mount rising 1,791 feet (546 meters) above sea level; the scene of the contest between Elijah and the priests of Baal

Mount Horeb also **Mount Sinai,** where God gave Moses the Ten Commandments

Mount of Olives a range of low hills east of Jerusalem; in the Bible, the mount from which Jesus made his triumphal entry into Jerusalem and where he spent much time in contemplation

Mount Sinai also **Mount Horeb,** where God gave Moses the Ten Commandments

multiply to increase in number as more and more children are born

multitude a large number of people or things

myrrh a bitter-tasting tree sap used as incense

Nabatean a member of an ancient Arabian people whose kingdom extended from Syria to the Persian Gulf

Nazareth a town in northern Palestine, a part of ancient Galilee; home of Joseph, Mary, and Jesus in his boyhood

Nehemiah during the reign of the Persians, a Jew who received permission from Persia's king to rebuild the walls of Jerusalem; when the restoration was complete, he also began a religious reform of the city

New Testament the part of the Bible which contains the life and teachings of Jesus as recorded by his followers, together with their own experiences and teachings

nigh near

Nile River the longest river in the world, rising near the equator and flowing into the Mediterranean Sea; the river in Egypt where

Moses' mother left him among the bulrushes in a basket to be found by Pharaoh's daughter

Nineveh the capital of the Assyrian empire and the city Jonah saved by warning its citizens of God's displeasure with their wicked ways

nomad a member of a tribe that moves from place to place to find food or pasture for herds and flocks

oasis a fertile spot in the desert where there is water and usually trees and other vegetation

offering the sacrifice of an animal to a god or goddess, usually a burnt sacrifice made on an altar

Old Testament the Bible's earlier and larger part containing the religious and social laws of the Hebrews, a record of their history, their important literature, and writings of their prophets

ordain to order; decide; pass a law; officially appoint a religious leader

overseer a person who directs the work of others

pagan a person who worships many gods or no gods; a heathen

Palestine also known as the Holy Land and the Land of Canaan, a small land at the eastern end of the Mediterranean Sea where both Judaism and Christianity originated; the site of many Biblical and historical events; in ancient times, an area ruled by many peoples, including the Egyptians, the Philistines, the Israelites, the Assyrians, the Babylonians, the Persians, and the Romans

Palm Sunday the Sunday before Easter Sunday, celebrated in memory of the triumphal entry of Jesus into Jerusalem, when palm branches were strewn before him

papyrus a tall water plant from which ancient peoples made a kind of paper on which to write; bulrush

parable a short story used to teach a lesson or truth

Paradise in some religions heaven, where God, the angels, and the righteous are; also Garden of Eden

Passover the annual, 8-day feast in memory of the Hebrews' escape from Egypt, where they had been slaves; named *Passover* from the story of the tenth plague God brought on Egypt, when God killed the firstborn of every Egyptian home but *passed over* the Israelite houses

Pella a city in eastern Palestine; in AD 66, the Christian community of Jerusalem fled to Pella after a warning that Jerusalem would be destroyed; an important church center since that time

Pentecost the Jewish thanksgiving feast for the harvest, observed about seven weeks after the Passover; the descent of the Holy Spirit upon the apostles after their nine days of prayer following Jesus' ascent into heaven; the Christian holiday celebrated the seventh Sunday after Easter honoring the descent of the Holy Spirit

perish to die

Persia the center of a vast empire and great civilization in the ancient world, extending from North Africa and southeastern Europe in the west to India in the east, and from the Gulf of Oman in the south to southern Russia in the north

pharaoh or **Pharaoh** the title given to the kings of ancient Egypt

Pharisee in the time of Christ, a member of a Jewish sect that was strict in keeping to tradition and the laws of its religion

Philippi a city of ancient Macedonia, the scene of one of the many arrests of the Apostle Paul

Philistine one of the warlike people of Philistia in southwestern Pales-

tine that attacked the Israelites many times
Phoenicia on the eastern Mediterranean, a great ancient kingdom famous for its exploration throughout the Mediterranean area and its general seafaring
Phrygia an ancient country in central and northwestern Asia Minor
pillar a strong, slender, upright structure; a column
plague any dangerous disease or other form of punishment thought to be sent by God
plain of Dura in ancient Babylon, the flat stretch of land where King Nebuchadnezzar set up his golden image for worship
plain of Gennesaret in ancient times, the name given to the stretch of land lying at the northwest corner of the Sea of Galilee; the spot where Jesus fed 5,000 persons with two fish and five loaves
pomegranate a somewhat sour-tasting, reddish-yellow fruit with a thick skin and many red seeds inside surrounded by juicy red pulp
pottage a thick soup of vegetables or of vegetables and meat
preacher one who speaks publicly on a religious subject; a minister
predict to announce or tell beforehand
preserve to keep from harm or change
prevail to be stronger; win the victory
priest a special servant of a god, one who performs certain public religious acts
proceedeth comes from
procurator, Roman an administrator of an ancient Roman province
prodigal wasteful; extravagant
Promised Land the country God is said to have promised to Abraham and his descendants; Canaan
prophecy something told about the future; an indication of events to come
prophet a person who preaches what he believes God has revealed to him
Prophet of the Highest John the Baptist
proverb a short, wise saying used for a long time by many people
provoke to make angry
psalm a sacred song or poem
publican a tax collector
pyramid any one of the massive stone structures that served as tombs for the ancient Egyptian royalty

quail any one of various plump game birds belonging to the same family as chickens and pheasants; the birds God sent the Israelites as food in the wilderness

rabbi a teacher of the Jewish religion; a leader of a Jewish congregation
reap to cut grain and gather a crop from, as when one harvests
Red Sea an arm of the Indian Ocean separating the Arabian Peninsula from northeastern Africa, said to have been parted by God so that Moses and the Israelites could cross unharmed
religion belief in God or gods; worship of God or gods
religious council also **Sanhedrin,** the great council of the ancient Jews, consisting of 71 members; having come into existence in a period of Greek domination over Israel, the final authority on all matters affecting the Jewish law; powers included arrest and trial, but not execution
rend to tear or rip
render to give
repent to feel sorry for having done wrong and to seek forgiveness for the offense
restore to bring back; reestablish

resurrection the rising of Jesus after his death and burial
righteous doing right; virtuous
righteousness upright conduct; virtue
ritual a ceremony such as a burnt sacrifice, a baptism, or a marriage
Rome also **Roman Empire,** a vast ancient empire that ruled Judea during the life of Jesus; the city of Rome was the capital of the Roman Empire

Sabaoth armies, hosts
Sabbath a day of the week used for rest and worship
sackcloth a coarse cloth worn as a sign of mourning or repentance
sackcloth and ashes, in referring to someone either mourning or repenting for wrongdoing by wearing a garment made of sackcloth and rubbing ashes into the garment and on the body
sacred holy
sacrifice the offering of an animal or thing to a goddess or a god, especially a burnt offering
Sadducee in the time of Christ, a member of the Jewish sect next to the Pharisees in power
salvation the act of saving the soul; deliverance from sin and from punishment for sin
Samaritan in the Old Testament, an individual belonging to the kingdom of Northern Israel; in the New Testament, inhabitants of the province of Samaria, whom the Jews in the time of Christ considered an inferior group religiously and socially
Satan the evil spirit; the enemy of goodness; the devil; especially in Christianity, the greatest enemy of God and humankind
savior also **saviour,** a person who rescues; a deliverer from harm
scornful looking down upon; despising
scorpion a kind of whip made of knotted cords with lead spikes
scribe in ancient times, a teacher of Jewish law
scroll a roll of paper or some other material, especially one with writing on it
Sea of Galilee a small freshwater lake in northern Palestine where Jesus taught and performed many miracles
sect a group of persons having the same principles, beliefs, or opinions
selah a Hebrew word occurring often in the psalms, perhaps a musical direction meaning "pause here"
Semite a member of the peoples speaking any of the Semitic languages, including the ancient Hebrews, the Phoenicians, and the Assyrians
seraph plural **seraphim,** one of the higher orders of angels, immediately above the cherubim; an angel of a warm, loving nature
Sermon on the Mount Jesus' sermon presenting his basic teachings, including the **Lord's Prayer** and the **Beatitudes**
serpent a snake, especially a big snake; in the Bible, often Satan
shepherd a person who takes care of sheep; a person who cares for and protects; a spiritual guide
shewbread the unleavened bread that the ancient Jewish priests placed near the altar every Sabbath as an offering to God
shrine an altar, small chapel, or other place of worship
sickle a tool with a short, curved blade on a short handle, used for cutting grass and the like
Silas a distinguished member of the Apostolic Church who accompanied the Apostle Paul both to Antioch and on his second missionary journey
sin to break the law of God

smite to strike a blow; to hit
Sodom and Gomorrah ancient, wicked cities near the Dead Sea that were said to have been destroyed by a fire from heaven
Son of God the Messiah
sore to a great extent; very
soul the part of the human being that thinks, feels, and makes the body act; the spiritual part of a person, distinct from the physical part; in many religions, in death the soul and body separate, and the soul lives forever
sow to plant
sphinx a statue of a lion's body with the head of a man, ram, or hawk; in ancient art, statues sometimes used to represent angels
stay the act of stopping; restraint
Stephen the first Christian martyr, stoned to death outside Jerusalem some time after the crucifixion
steward a person in charge of food and table service for a gathering, such as a feast
suckling a very young child or animal, especially one still nursing
suffer to allow; permit
sun dial an instrument for telling the time of day by the position of a shadow cast by the sun
swaddling clothes long, narrow strips of cloth, in Jesus' time used for wrapping a newborn baby in order to prevent its free movement
swine hogs or pigs
synagogue a building or place that Jews use for worship and religious instruction; a temple

tablet a small, smooth piece of stone or other material used in ancient times to write or draw on
Tarsus the large capital city of the Roman province of Cilicia, in Asia Minor; the birthplace of the Apostle Paul
temple a building used for the service or worship of a god or gods
Temple of Jerusalem also **Temple of Solomon,** a temple King Solomon built in Jerusalem, starting about 966 BC, in honor of God; construction lasted seven or eight years; gold and silver used to decorate this building may have been worth as much as $250 million
tempt to try to make someone do something; to test
temptation the act of making or trying to make someone do something; a test
Ten Commandments the ten rules for living and for worship that God is said to have given to Moses on Mount Sinai
tree of the knowledge of good and evil the forbidden tree in the Garden of Eden from which Adam and Eve ate, causing God to banish them forever from Paradise
tribe a group of persons forming a community and claiming descent from a common ancestor
twelve tribes of Israel the twelve divisions of the ancient Hebrews, each claiming descent from a son of Jacob

unleavened bread flat bread, made without yeast or any other substance that would cause the dough to rise
Uz an ancient land believed to have been located in the Syrian desert; the home of Job

vain as **in vain,** without sense or wisdom; foolishly; senselessly
vanity too much pride in one's looks, ability, or accomplishments
vaunteth brags
vision something seen in the imagination, in a dream, in one's thoughts, or the like
vizier a high government official in ancient Egypt, as a minister of state
void an empty space

wanderer one who moves here and there with no special purpose
waterpot a vessel, usually of earthenware, for holding and storing water
whence from where
wilderness a wild place; a region with no one living in it
wise men also magi, the priests of an ancient Persian religion, famed as astrologers; belonging to this group were the Three Wise Men said to have followed a star to Bethlehem to find the newly born Jesus
worship to pay great honor and respect to, as to worship God
wrath anger

yoke something that joins or unites; a bond or tie

zeal eager desire or effort
Zion a hill in Jerusalem on which the Temple of Jerusalem and the royal palace stood; Israel or the Israelites; heaven; the Christian church

Bible sources

Editor's note: See glossary introduction for how to use this reference section.

Adam and Eve God creates the universe *(Gen. 1);* God casts Adam and Eve forever from Eden *(Gen. 2–3)*
Cain and Abel Cain murders his brother Abel; God punishes Cain *(Gen. 4)*
Noah and the ark God saves Noah and his family from the flood *(Gen. 6–9:17)*
The Tower of Babel God scatters humanity and creates many languages *(Gen. 11:1–9)*
Abraham, father of nations the later life of Abraham, when he becomes father of the Israelite people *(Gen. 12–18, Gen. 20–21)*
Lot's escape: Sodom and Gomorrah God destroys two wicked cities but spares Abraham's nephew Lot *(Gen. 19:1–30)*
Abraham's sacrifice: A proof of faith God commands that Abraham burn his son Isaac as a sacrifice *(Gen. 22:1–18)*
Isaac and Rebecca Abraham's son marries a girl from his father's own tribe *(Gen. 24)*
Jacob tricks his brother Esau Jacob steals Esau's birthright and flees for safety *(Gen. 25:27–34, Gen. 27)*
Jacob's ladder to heaven God promises to protect Jacob, now homeless *(Gen. 28:11–22)*
Jacob's new family Jacob marries *(Gen. 29:1–28)*
The angel and Jacob: A wrestling match Jacob struggles for an angel's blessing *(Gen. 32:24–32)*
Betrayal: Joseph becomes a slave Joseph's jealous brothers sell him into slavery *(Gen. 37)*
Joseph, guardian of Egypt Joseph becomes a high official in the Egyptian court *(Gen. 39–41:44)*
Joseph tests his brothers Joseph and his brothers reunite *(Gen. 42–45)*
Moses, the Hebrew child Moses grows up as an Egyptian but finally must flee *(Exod. 2);* God commands Moses to return to Egypt and free the Hebrew slaves *(Exod. 3–4:20)*
Moses and Pharaoh: A test of power God visits plagues on Egypt; Pharaoh lets the Hebrews go *(Exod. 5–13)*

Israel faces the wilderness God protects and feeds Moses and the Israelites as they journey to Mount Sinai *(Exod. 14–16:31)*

The Ten Commandments on Mount Sinai, God gives Moses the Ten Commandments *(Exod. 19–20)*; Israelites sin, worshipping the golden calf *(Exod. 32)*

Joshua wins at Jericho Joshua takes Jericho during his conquest of Palestine *(Josh. 2–3, Josh. 6)*

Gideon, valiant warrior Gideon frees the Israelites from the Midianites' domination *(Judg. 6–7)*

Samson's secret strength a powerful Israelite—whose strength comes from his long hair—fights the Philistines, then dies destroying their temple *(Judg. 13–16)*

Ruth: A story of love God rewards a young widow for sacrificing her own security to aid her helpless mother-in-law *(Ruth 1–4)*

David, from shepherd to king a shepherd boy defeats the Philistine giant, Goliath *(1 Sam. 17)* and becomes a great king of Israel *(1 Sam. 18–31, 2 Sam. 1–5:3)*

Solomon, wise and wealthy ruler Solomon's reign begins with his building the Temple of Jerusalem *(1 Kings 1–8)* and ends with God's punishment for Solomon's greed and other offenses *(1 Kings 11)*

Jeroboam, divided Israel's foolish king Jeroboam takes northern Israel from Solomon's son; God later punishes Jeroboam for worshipping pagan idols *(1 Kings 11–15)*

Elijah, defender of God Elijah, a prophet, successfully opposes Queen Jezebel's pagan worship of Baal *(1 Kings 17, 18:19–45)*

Good Hezekiah, King of Judah by turning back a sun dial, God adds years to Hezekiah's life so he can keep guiding his people *(2 Kings 18–21)*

Jonah and the great fish a great fish swallows Jonah after he refuses to do as God commands, instead running away to the sea; finally, Jonah obeys God *(Jon. 1–4)*

Ezekiel, captive priest of Babylon Ezekiel, an exiled priest, sees a vision sent from God *(Ezek. 1–3:14)* and becomes a prophet of the exiled Israelites *(Ezek. 4–48)*

Job's faith destruction and death come to Job's family *(Job 1–2)*; throughout his suffering, though weakened, Job keeps his trust in the Lord, and God restores Job's good fortune *(Job 3–42)*

Three Holy Children survive the furnace King Nebuchadnezzar throws Shadrach, Meshach, and Abednego into a fiery furnace; their faith saves them *(Dan. 3)*

Daniel in the lions' den Daniel's faith in God saves him when King Darius has him thrown into a den of hungry lions *(Dan. 6)*

John, Prophet of the Messiah John the Baptist's birth *(Luke 1:5–25, Luke 1:57–80)*

Baby Jesus lights up the world the birth of Jesus *(Matt. 1:18–25, 2:1–12; Luke 1:26–38, 2:1–20)*

Young Jesus Jesus' family flees to Egypt, returning when Herod dies; Jesus at the temple in Jerusalem, speaking with the rabbis *(Matt. 2:13–23; Luke 2:21–52)*

John, preacher in the wilderness John preaches of the Messiah, baptizes Jesus *(Matt. 3; Mark 1:1–11; Luke 3:2–22; John 1:15–36)*

John dies a prisoner Herod's wife and step-daughter bring about John the Baptist's execution *(Matt. 14:1–12; Mark 6:17–29; Luke 7:19–28)*

Jesus triumphs over Satan in the wilderness, Jesus resists Satan's temptation *(Matt. 4:1–11; Mark 1:12–13; Luke 4:1–13)*

Cana: Jesus' first miracle Jesus turns water into wine *(John 2:1–11)*

Because he loved: Jesus' miracles Jesus feeds the multitudes *(Matt. 14:14–21; Mark 6:34–44; Luke 9:13–17; John 6:2–13)*; walks on water *(Matt. 14:22–33; Mark 6:45–51; John 6:14–21)*; and performs other miracles *(Matt. 9:18–34: Mark 5; Luke 8:27–56)*

Jesus' teachings: Words to live by beware of hypocrites *(Matt. 16; Mark 7:1–9)*; the temptations of riches *(Matt. 19:21–24; Mark 10:23–29; Luke 18:22–30)*; render unto Caesar *(Matt. 22:17–22; Mark 12:14–17; Luke 20:22–26)*; and the stoning of the unfaithful wife *(John 8:2–11)*

The Good Samaritan the meaning of "good neighbor": a parable *(Luke 10:30–37)*

The Prodigal Son the meaning of forgiveness: the parable of the wasteful son *(Luke 15:4–32)*

The Unkind Servant the meaning of forgiveness: the parable of the pitiless servant *(Matt. 18:21–35)*

Sermon on the Mount Jesus teaches how to be a good Christian *(Matt. 5–7; Luke 6)*; the Beatitudes *(Matt. 5:3–11)*; the Lord's Prayer *(Matt. 6:9–13)*; Jesus speaks with Moses and Elijah *(Matt. 17:1–5; Mark 9:1–6; Luke 9:28–35)*

Jesus raises Lazarus from death *(John 11:1–46)*

Judas betrays Jesus the apostle arranges to deliver Jesus to the high priests *(Matt. 26:1–15; Mark 14:1–11; Luke 22:1–6; John 12:1–8)*

Palm Sunday Jesus enters Jerusalem triumphantly *(Matt. 21:1–11; Mark 11:1–10; Luke 19:29–44; John 12:9–18)*; Jesus chases the money changers from the temple *(Matt. 21:12–17; Mark 11:15–18; Luke 19:45–48)*

The Last Supper Jesus and the apostles celebrate the Passover Feast, the eve of the crucifixion *(Matt. 26:17–35; Mark 14:12–31; Luke 22:7–34; John 13)*

Gethsemane: Soldiers arrest Jesus Judas betrays Jesus with a kiss *(Matt. 26:36–58; Mark 14:32–54; Luke 22:39–54; John 18:1–12)*

A sentence of death for Jesus the religious council hears Jesus' case; Peter denies Jesus; Pilate condemns Jesus *(Matt. 26:59–75, 27:1–31; Mark 14:55–72, 15:1–20; Luke 22:55–71, 23:1–25; John 18:13–40, 19:1–16)*

The cross soldiers lead Jesus to Calvary; he is crucified and dies *(Matt. 27:32–56; Mark 15:21–41; Luke 23:26–49; John 19:17–36)*

The Risen Christ Joseph of Arimathea and Nicodemus see to Jesus' burial; the apostles hear Jesus has risen; the Risen Christ appears; Christ ascends to heaven *(Matt. 27:57–66, Matt. 28; Mark 15:42–47, Mark 16; Luke 23:50–56, Luke 24; John 19:37–42, John 20–21)*

Paul, missionary of Christ the Pharisee Saul becomes the Apostle Paul and helps to spread Christianity throughout the Mediterranean *(Acts 9:1–30; Acts 13–14, 16:19–40, 21:28–36, 23:7–33)*

Index

Old Testament

New Testament